My Hope for Tomorrow
Ruby Dhal

Written and arranged by Ruby Dhal

Cover Design © Randeep Singh Sohal

(@artful_skecha)
Interior Design © Mitch Green
(@radpresspublishing)

www.rubydhal.com

To my family,
You will always be my home.

Believe me when I tell you, days like this will pass too.

Dear reader, *this one is for you.*

I have written countless poems over the past few years as I pushed forward in my healing journey. Pieces about love, heartbreak and healing. Pieces about survival. Pieces about moving forward in the face of chaos and coming to grips with my place in this world. But the pieces that have continuously found a supple place inside my heart have been the ones that we, you and I, have felt together. The pieces that make you feel understood are the ones that make me feel understood too. They make me feel as though I am not alone in my happiness or grief, as though there is hope for me and every other person who dreams that one day they can roar from the depths of despair.

Because there is hope.

Without hope and love we would be searching frantically for a way to lessen the pain, and still being unable to. Love has the power to cure every ache and hurt caused by our experiences – and this starts with self-love.

My hope for you is that you find parts of yourself in these pages, parts that are not only able to ease your sorrow but also help you on your healing journey.

My hope for you is to become stronger in the face of the obstacles ahead of you and for you to accept your scars, because they make you undeniably beautiful. My hope for you is to start anew after uncovering yourself through this book, after peeling off every layer of your emotions, after accepting and growing and learning, and then taking a step towards self-love and happiness.

My hope for tomorrow is that my words act as a balm to the gentle throbbing in your chest, just as your presence soothes the throbbing in mine. We are on our journeys to heal together. You are never alone, and I hope that you remember this – every single day from today.

Love, Ruby Dhal x

The healing begins…

A Miracle

When I look at you, I see someone who shines with strength and resilience. I see a human being who has experienced so much pain in a short span of a life that it is unbelievable that you became this way. It is unbelievable how you can be this kind, this giving and filled with enough care for others that sometimes you fall short of loving yourself. Sometimes I am unable to comprehend what made you this person. Was it pain, anguish or the loss of loved ones? What is it that keeps you going, despite it all? Despite every obstruction and each difficult decision that you have had to make, how can you continue to be a wonderful soul that everyone wants a piece of? I cannot understand it. I just cannot.

Because when I look at you, I see endless nights of tear-soaked pillows and a lifetime of shoulders burdened with lessons that made you wiser than your years. When I look at you, I see a person coupled with enough warmth that whoever touches your presence no longer feels cold. When I look at you, I see a person filled with the kind of wisdom that will help generations to come. When I look at you, I see a heart of gold and a soul yearning to be loved.

When I look at you, I see a warrior, a fighter – someone who did not let themselves stay broken for too long. But sometimes I am unable to comprehend how, despite it all, you became this way. Because when I look at you, I see an unimaginable human being. I see a miracle.

Love (Part I)

Love is not supposed to feel like pain. Like there is a stone rammed so hard inside your chest that even breathing hurts. Love is not supposed to break you into a thousand pieces at night, only to meet you in the morning and break you more. Or make you feel like everything in your life is over and you have nowhere to go. Like those nights when you will do anything to stop hurting, to make it all go away. Love is not supposed to make you feel worthless. No.

Love is supposed to build you, you should grow with the person that you love – not diminish. Love should not kill your soul but fill you with life. Love is not supposed to feel like you have daggers twisting in your heart and tears as proof on your cheeks. No. Love is supposed to feel like the wind that allows you to fly. Love is supposed to soften you, not turn you into stone. Love is supposed to show you that you are worth everything, not nothing. No. It is not love if all it ever does is cause you pain. I refuse to believe that.

You are not supposed to love someone so much that it hurts – you just aren't. Think about it – if you were then no one would want to fall in love. Love is not hurt, it is the kind of balm that fills you with so much tenderness that you learn to live again. That is what love is. That is what love always is.

Because when I look at you, I see an
unimaginable
human being. *I see a miracle.*

The Honest Truth

Unfortunately, at least once in your life you will hurt someone very deeply, even if you do not want to. You will have to look into their eyes and tell them a truth that could potentially break them. But you will do it anyway because deep down you will know that despite the hurt your truth will cause, it will have the potential to create so much goodness later in their life.

I know that a lot of us feel guilty when we cause someone pain – either by telling them something that will affect them or carrying out an action that they do not like. It makes us feel bad because we are good human beings, aren't we? And good human beings do not hurt others, do they? Essentially, how good or bad you are is not determined by a small act of hurtfulness that you cause but would like to avoid. Because unfortunately, we all play a part in the hard lessons that other people learn – even if we do not want to. I know that you do not want to hurt someone, even though that will help them learn a valuable lesson in their life, and you know that causing them pain will make you look bad – in your eyes and theirs. And perhaps they will feel broken beyond repair during the initial weeks or months of their grief.

I guess the only way to deal with this is to accept pain-giving as proof of you being human – imperfect and flawed in many beautifully tragic ways. Another way to deal with it is to accept that destiny is working in their favour, to make sure that everything will eventually work out for the person whom you have hurt. Therefore, the pain that you cause them is what allows them to become stronger and the best version of themselves. Yes, we would like to avoid hurting others and getting hurt too. But in the fluctuating pattern of life that involves learning, as well as teaching lessons, we get broken and we in turn break others and there is nothing we can do to change it. All we can do is accept it, all we can do is hope that the pain will turn into something positive one day. All we can do is try to be as good to people as we can, even when we are hurting them.

No Regrets

The truth is – I still do not regret you.

Meeting you was one of the best things that has ever happened to me. You brought positivity, love and sunshine into my life. You showed me how to see the world in a different way altogether, and you made me stronger, wiser and kinder. You showed me that my dreams were valid, and you made me realize my worth. And the best part is – you did not do any of these things on purpose, they just happened. Me changing this much was a by-product of our friendship, of everything that you could do by just being there.

And I will always be grateful to you for that. You allowed me to develop a better mindset and you added incredible value to me as someone who can contribute to the wellbeing of those around them. You showed me that one person has the power to make your whole life beautiful. You allowed me to grow in several ways and they were all for the best. So, even if there was no place in this world for us and you did not feel the same way – you were one of the best things that ever happened to me. And because of this, I can never regret you.

Regardless

Do not let someone else's negativity cloud your mind, and do not let their perception of life constrain yours. It is true that everyone is a reflection of their experiences, they have grown and changed and altered because of the years they left behind. However, it is up to you whether you reflect light or darkness. You choose whether you want your bad experiences to build you and you choose whether it is the good. People can only break us as much as we let them. We are the one whose opinions and choices matter, not them.

Do not lose your self-worth because of another person's distorted perception of you. Their opinions do not determine your value – only yours do. You are someone who has the potential to be complete in yourself. You do not need another person to tell you whether you are worth caring about, or investing time into, or loving. Because you should already know that you are worth not only love but a lot more. So, continue working on yourself and continue believing in yourself, and never stop loving the person that you are growing into each day.

Regardless of what others say. Regardless of what others do.

Love is the kind of happiness that fills you with so much warmth that you learn *to live again*.

Easy love

I wish love was easy. I wish I could say that in life you will magically meet someone whom you will fall in love with, and they will love you too and you both will live happily ever after. And sometimes, that is the case. I wish that it was the case all the time, but it is not. You are bound to fall in love time and time again for people who are not good for you, for people who do not value you as much as they should, for people who do not want you even though you would give the world to them. And there will come a time when they will want you, but your heart will no longer beat for them, where you will try and try but your feelings will not develop, and you will have no other choice than to break their heart.

I wish things were simple. I wish life was simple. But it is not. Life is complicated and relationships even more so. We hurt others and get hurt and we shatter more often than not, but it is not all for nothing. We grasp truths about life and teach others many truths too and, through it all, we grow and grow until we become the best version of ourselves. Yes, we will make mistakes. Yes, we will continue to get hurt and do a little hurting as well. But we are human, and we are constantly growing and learning from our mistakes.

I wish relationships were easy. I wish life was easier. But it is not, and the best way to grasp it all is to accept the bad parts and soak in all the good. The best way to live through the heartache and every trouble in life is to become stronger, and to learn to accept that things will not always go the way we want them to, but sometimes they will, and it is those little moments of happiness and love that we must live for. I wish love was easy, but it is not. Love is like holding a bucketload of struggles as you stride forward, driving you to the brink of confusion, but then the bucket gets lighter as the struggles pour into the road one by one, and you rise with a surety of yourself that manages to silence any self-doubt that you had. You no longer question whether you deserve love because you know that you do. You no longer think about what love means because the difficult path that you took has taught you everything that you had to know, the path that you took has shown you what love is and what it is not.

And that is what makes love the most beautiful experience in the world. That is what allows us to want it in our lives and that is what makes us appreciate love more and more.

What Hurts the Most

And do you know what hurts the most – thinking that we cannot share our pain. What hurts the most is being aware that there is not a single person who has not experienced sorrow but living as though none of us have. What hurts the most is not being able to talk to each other about our scars. What hurts the most is believing that we will not be able to find someone who might empathise with our feelings, just because of our assumptions that others cannot comprehend what we go through. What hurts the most is thinking that our different experiences make us incapable of easing each other's aching hearts, because that is not true.

Believe me when I say that a friend can be found in every individual who has undergone pain, and believe me when I say that you will not find a single person who has not experienced a little bit of it. What hurts the most is thinking that you are alone in your journey when you are not. There are ears willing to listen to your problems and shoulders willing to give your heart all the rest that it needs. What hurts the most is fearing that we must go through things on our own. Because believe me when I say that you are not alone in what you experience and when I say that you can find a companion in me, or him, or her or anyone who has a heart beating inside their chest. What hurts the most is bottling up your feelings inside your soul rather than letting them pour down your cheeks.

What hurts the most is being quiet when all you want to do is scream.

Believe me when I say that I will hear your cries and I will comfort your spirit in times of need. And believe me when I say that there are kinder souls in the world than you think. All you need to do is trust someone. All you need to do is acknowledge that they will be there for you. All you need to do is take a small step forward. And what hurts most of all – when you try so hard to cage your emotions when all they want is to be set free.

Self-Love

You spent so many years trying to figure out what self-love meant, only to find it on a cold December night as you counted stars in an empty sky that did not give you any wishes but only rain. Your shoulders were slumped with the weight of a lifetime of worries that would take another lifetime to unravel. You looked at your reflection in the mirror and it all finally made sense – it was you.

It was you who held your own hand and wiped your tears. It was you who picked up your broken pieces – to mend them, to heal. It was you who hugged yourself to sleep at night when the arms of lost lovers were too strong to comfort the softness within you. It was always you. And it was this realisation that allowed you to raise your shoulders high one last time, to look inside your eyes – once a warm brown, now withered – and smile in a way that told you it would all be okay. It was when you realized that no matter who left, you would always stay, no matter who hurt you, you would find a way to heal again. You would always be there for yourself. That is when you learned what self-love meant.

It was you, and it was always going to be you in the end.

All you need to do is *trust someone.* All you
need to do is accept that they will understand
you. All you need to do is take *a small step
forward.*

Loneliness

Sometimes loneliness does not crawl in as a restless night, but it comes in the form of people. The kind that you stumble upon over a light-hearted conversation about how funny they looked with an emoji on Snapchat, or the kind that you spend years unpeeling only to realize that their deepest parts, the ones capable of stirring not just a storm, but a heartbreak, tears and a whole lot of healing within you, were hidden all along. Sometimes loneliness is not felt in silence, but in a loud bustling room filled with people who cannot do anything to take your emptiness away. Sometimes loneliness is the shadow that follows you on the brightest day of the year because you do not feel as happy as others do, and you always think that something is wrong with you because of it. Sometimes loneliness is the quietness that trails through the thin gap under your front door after a busy day and sometimes, just sometimes, loneliness comes from the people that you love.

Loneliness is not always felt, but it is there at the back of your mind – just like every memory they left behind is. But most of the time, loneliness is there on nights when you have only yourself to speak to. That is when loneliness hits you the most. That is when loneliness kills.

Human-sized Hole

It is hard to accept that you could come across countless people in your life, but only a few manage to touch you – and I mean truly touch you. Only a few people can grab hold of your heart in a way you never imagined. Only a few people can delve inside your soul through your eyes in an instant. It is odd to think that you could know someone for years and they still do not know who you truly are, and you could know someone for just a few weeks, but they manage to find out your deepest, darkest secrets without you having to say a thing. These people only come occasionally, often once in a whole lifetime, but you end up spending the rest of your life thinking about how their presence turned your whole world around. You spend the remaining time after their departure trying, and failing, to find traces of them in others.

These kind of people are both a blessing and a curse. They fill your life with so much sunshine, positivity and light that life without them feels grim. They make you so happy that you do not know what it is like to feel pain. But when they leave, because believe me when I say that sunlight never stays in one place, there is a human-side hole inside your chest that you spend the rest of your life trying to fill.

Yesterday, Today and Tomorrow

You are so much more than this.

More than the emptiness, the confusion, and those days when you feel lost and alone. More than the long, painful nights where you dig your face into your damp pillow, more than the anxiety about the future and what it holds. More than the experiences that broke you down time and time again, more than the lost friendships and lovers that left and never looked back. More than the lessons you learned and those you chose to ignore, more than the regrets you firmly hold onto, in fear that you will make those mistakes again.

More than the fights, the hurt and the anguish, and more than the anxiety about where your life is headed. More than the displacement that settles inside you when you realize that you have nothing figured out. More than the scars, the heartbreak, the broken homes, more than the dreams that you could not complete and the challenges you could not uphold. You are so much more than this. More than yesterday's lessons and today's experiences, and so much more than what tomorrow will have in store.

Sometimes *loneliness is the shadow* that
follows you on the brightest day of the year.

What Saved Me

I have reached a point in my life where nothing hurts me as badly as it used to. Things happen, you get hurt, people leave, and hearts get broken – but life goes on. I have built a wall around me using nothing but self-love and that is why when things go wrong, I am no longer affected. I love myself enough now to know my worth, and that means not crying about someone who did not love me enough to stay, or fight for me when they should have.

I used to be the kind of person who would be affected by the smallest things, despite having undergone so much in such a short period of time. And now, I cannot shed a single tear. This is not because I have become numb, but because I know no one is worth my tears. I used to think that nothing gets better, and that things can only get worse and some of us are destined for just pain. But I was wrong. Things do get better and that is all I keep close to me now. The tiniest glimmer of hope and possibility – the fact that there is always light at the end of the tunnel and no matter what anyone says, things get better with time. Believe me, they do.

And even if it appears that things do not get better with time, you earn enough strength to deal with them and that is still progress, that is still a step in the right direction. Even though sometimes it feels as though life has not moved forward and you are still in the same place – hurting, cracking your heart open and losing people over and over again – you are not the same person you were the first time that you experienced loss. You are different. You have grown in many ways and you have gained the kind of strength that was not there before. Sometimes, that is all you need – hope that things change for the best. Therefore, things do not hurt me as much as they used to. I have managed to believe in the light when before there was none, I have realized that only I have the power to protect myself. And most importantly, I have learned to do the one thing that we all find so difficult to do – I have learned to love myself in ways that I never thought possible, and this is what saved me.

This Generation

The worst thing about the way our generation views relationships are our expectations – we just have too many. We expect things that perhaps will not be met, and when those expectations are not satisfied, we assume that the love no longer exists. When we initially meet someone, our heart races at 100 miles an hour, but then we expect that this feeling will exist throughout the relationship, and that is not the case. We need to get rid of this assumption that love will always feel like how it did when we first fell into – with fireworks in our body.

Love does not need to race at 100 miles all the time, it is not always going to cause crazy jitters inside your stomach or make you feel as though you are on top of the world. Love can be quiet and calm too. Love can be in the silence that you share together, or in the warmth of each other's embrace. Love continues in your arguments, your fights, your tears, and those days of calm when you do not know what to do or where to go. Love continues in your friendship, and in your conversations. Just because love does not cause butterflies in your stomach the way it did when you first met your partner, it does not mean that love no longer exists. There is absolutely nothing wrong with love being soft and unspoken, slow and steady.

It is easy to fall in love. It is easy to have fireworks in the beginning, followed by unrealistic expectations that they will always stay. It is much more difficult to understand that there will be hiccups. It is even harder to understand that love is constantly changing and with time it will not feel like how it did when you first fell into it. But gradually, you need to learn to change yourself alongside it.

Waiting

Life waits for no one. You realize this as you watch past lovers fold into new relationships and walk on different journeys without you. You realize this as you watch people graduate, start jobs, get married and move countries. You realize this as weeks turn into months and months into years and hello turns into *I have not seen you for a while,* and friendship turns into love and love into something more – or maybe nothing.

Life waits for no one. You realize this as the hurt that filled your heart has finally spilled out, making room for nothing but love. You realize this as you look at yourself in the mirror and notice the lines that touched your eyes have now moved to the edges of your mouth, because all you do is smile these days. You realize this as the sadness starts to fade and a gentleness hugs you, making room for adventures you never thought you would have, making room for people you never thought you would be able to fit inside your soul, making room for a feeling you never thought you would experience again.

Life waits for no one. You realize this as you get up each morning with a determined smile, counting your blessings in the form of people and adventures and all your achievements. Life waits for no one. And you realize this when those who broke you finally return to the place where they had left you, only to realize that you were never standing there waiting for them.

The best way to live through heartache and
every trouble in life is to *become stronger,* and
to learn to accept that things will not always go
the way we want them to, but sometimes they
will, and it is those little moments of happiness
and love *that we must live for.*

The Plan

Meeting people is never an accident. Someone cannot walk in and out of your life without reason. Lessons and the growth that you experience are never spontaneous. *It is always meant to be.* There is a higher purpose, an end beyond you and I, which we will never know until we reach it. So, I want you to stop treating your experiences as casual occurrences that randomly took place and start looking for a deeper meaning, an end or a goal. Something that helps you flourish, that teaches you the important lessons that only people and their existence can provide you.

There is a plan – and you must find it if you want to conquer it. Think about it, in a world consisting of over 7.53 billion people, each capable of teaching you something – why did your path cross with this person? It was because you needed a particular lesson at this point in your life. Think about it deeply, only then will you stop treating your growth as an accident and start appreciating it as a beautiful journey meant just for you.

Love (Part 2)

I hope you find a love that gives you the strength to love yourself. A love that not only heals you but allows you to help heal others. A love that does not question you and breaks down every uncertainty you had about yourself. A love that teaches you that you are worth loving and you should never think otherwise. I hope you find a love that guides you as you walk towards your dreams and breaks away every barrier that you must face. I hope you find a love that makes you stronger, wiser and kinder. A love that only brings you down to build you up in ways you never imagined. I hope you find a love that becomes the light, and the reason for which you shine. A love that does not destroy you if it leaves. A love that believes in you, a love that shelters you and allows you to feel free.

I hope you find a lover who is your best friend, your companion and your equal in every way. A lover who would never leave you, but if they did then you would still be okay, because they will be the kind of lover who will teach you that you are not incomplete without them. I hope you find a lover who lets you feel whole and does not turn you weak. A lover who shows you your worth and teaches you to put yourself first. A lover who cherishes your soul instead of your body. I hope you find a lover who is as kind as the wind, as soft as feathers and as bright as sunlight.

I hope you find love within this lover and I hope that one day they find you too.

Home

I built a home in you, without knowing that I would not have a garden with sunflowers, a swing and green grass, but only withered trees. Without knowing that the windows would always be kept open to let the cold in, and at night there would be no blankets, or cuddles, or sleep. I built a home in you, without knowing that the floor was not enough to hold the weight of my love, and that the walls were not enough to keep me safe from the discomfort of the hollow shell that was your heart.

I built a home in you, without knowing that I would be the only one staying there because you had found yourself another place. I built a home in you, without knowing that it could not carry every part of me, without knowing that I was too much for it – or maybe, it was too little for me. I built a home in you, without knowing that homes are created with people and not within them, and that coming home to you would leave me empty inside. Because that is why, even after I built a home in you, I felt like I had no home in which to live.

It was you who hugged yourself to sleep at night,
when the arms of lost lovers were too strong to
comfort the softness within you.
It was always you.

Acceptance

I know how difficult it is – to keep experiencing things that have the power to break you to such an extent that you can feel the pain in your bones. But still, you tell others that you can deal with everything, and that you can cope with whatever life throws at you. I know how hard it is to continue being strong, despite it all. And sometimes, you just need a break from it all, so you can cry until your heart feels lighter – but you think that you will look weak if you accept it. But can you not see – it is not your strength that helps you heal every time, it is the softness of your soul.

You deal with every obstacle in your life with the kind of ease that tells tales of years of growth. You are a warm-hearted person, which means that you hurt a lot more, you feel a lot more and you care a lot more. So, you need to stop telling them and yourself that you are fine, even when you are not. Because, sometimes the pain should just take its toll. Cry, if you must, accept the hurt and the regret that comes with it. Because I know how hard it is to keep smiling through the pain, especially when all you want is a shoulder to rest your head on and someone's arms to hold.

Unrequited Love

You will not find answers in the arms of those who do not love you. There is no safe haven, no *I love you's* that cause a heat inside your chest, and no dreams of a future together. There are only hopeless promises sent out in one direction, to never be returned, there are desolate nights and a loneliness that even their presence cannot fill because they are never with you in the way that you want them to be. The only thing you will find are expressions of love that disappear the moment they leave your mouth. You will find eyes that can never reflect your face, no matter how much you search for yourself in them. You will find heartache, tears, uncertainty, incomplete actions, hopeful tomorrows, broken friendships and a lifetime of *what ifs*. You will find yourself alone at every corner because they will not come with you.

You will not find love in those people. All you will find is an emptiness that seeps in where love was supposed to and never leaves. All you will find is waiting, hoping, and wishing that they love you too. But you will not find love there, believe me, you will not find love there.

Losing You

I have reached a point where I am not surprised anymore. I am not surprised by the way some people treat me, or how low they can get. Promises are broken, and I am not fazed. People change their mind, more often than not, and I am not shaken. Sometimes they do not promise you anything, in fact, they do the opposite by telling you *'Do not have any expectations',* and that is what confuses me the most. I laugh at it, because a person can treat you as though you mean the world to them but then brush it off in an instant, as though it did not mean a thing.

However, I keep telling myself that I have experienced it once, so I can experience it again. I have experienced it once, so I can experience it a hundred times more and not weaken, because no one can hurt me as much as the first time. And I guess that is why I am at a point where losing people is no longer as heart breaking as it used to be. Because when you stop giving people parts of yourself, losing them no longer means that you are losing you.

Sometimes things need to end before new beginnings can arise, sometimes people need to break so that they can truly heal, and sometimes *love needs to leave* before it can return in a different way. *In the right way.*

The One

Let me be the one. The one you recite jokes that you cannot finish without laughing to. The one who knows what your favourite drink at your local café is. The one who makes you jam and butter toast, because one is too bland and the other too sweet, but together they balance each other. The one who watches your favourite TV shows with you and keeps the first book that made you feel alive on their bookshelf. The one who joins you in the car; our voices louder than the music as we sing along to a song that we both love. The one who can hold you on days when you feel most alone and nights when sleep is long gone.

Let me be the one. The one you can turn to whenever you have a problem. The one who does not always have a solution, but never stops giving you their shoulder to rest your head on. The one you can tell your crazy fantasies to, unashamed of how they make you look, because you know that I would never judge you. The one you can spend hours cuddling on the couch – unafraid of how hard your heart beats against my chest, unafraid of how vulnerable that makes you feel. Let me be the one. The one who can love you irrevocably. The one whom you can trust with all your pieces. The one who can show you just how magical you are to me, every single day for the rest of our lives.

The Chase

We live in a generation where chasing one another is seen as more desirable than walking side by side. A generation where, if a girl does not feign disinterestedness, or a guy is not wanted by many others, then we do not feel as attracted to them as we would otherwise have been. A generation where a girl is unconsciously tuned to play a *hard to get* tactic with a guy whom she wants to speak to, and where a guy must spend all his time and energy pursuing her until she cracks. Why can we not have conversations like normal people and be ourselves? Honest, upfront, and friends before anything else. Why, despite being adults, do we engage in playing games with one another to test each other out before we decide to 'commit' or 'let it be'.

If I find someone's company comforting, then I will spend time with them. If a person interests me, then I will speak to them. If their humour attracts me then I will laugh out loud and I will not have a care in the world about how it makes me look to those who abide by this law of *feign disinterestedness*. I will not indulge in frivolous games of pretending to be too busy to speak with them to keep them interested, until they truly get to know me and realize that the distanced person that I was pretending to be was not me.

If I am talkative then I will speak with you about everything and anything. If I am friendly, then I will be nice to you. I will not pretend to be rude or paint an attitude that does not exist within me just because girls who speak a lot, are loud, kind and sensitive are not your type. And I request you too to stop portraying yourself as the 'wanted by many and speaking to none' kind of person just to appear desirable to me. Because believe me – honesty is what I find most attractive. Do not chase me, and do not expect me to chase you. Walk with me, as a friend, or perhaps as something more. Let us take this journey together. Slowly. Step by step. Pace with pace. But together.

You are so much more than this. More
than yesterday's experiences and today's lessons,
and *so much more* than what tomorrow will
have in store.

Thank You

I want to thank you for being a wonderful dream that I almost touched. I want to thank you for showing me that an incredible human being can come into your life and change it in ways you never imagined. Thank you for allowing me to realize that people like you exist – kind-hearted, genuine souls who feel like sunshine on the darkest day of the year. People who only know how to love and spread smiles everywhere they go. Thank you for teaching me that angels exist in human form, and that the luckiest individuals are those who meet them. Thank you for making me feel lucky, even if it was for a short period.

Thank you for being the most magnificent person that I came across, because I know that I will probably never meet someone like you again. You will be a beautiful lesson that I am glad I learned. You will always be a part of me, because that is the only way that I can move on. That is the only way that I can keep your memories without hurting. That is the only way that I can continue walking without stumbling, that is the only way that I can stop my heart from breaking – by holding on to you.

I want to thank you for being you, because they do not make people like you anymore, and I hope you know that.

Goodbye (Part I)

I wish it was not difficult to say goodbye, I really do. I wish you could look this person in the eye and say goodbye, as though it does not mean anything. As though, after saying it you will not lose the one thing that makes you so happy, so relentlessly happy. And I wish that your goodbye did not entail them leaving, but instead it made them want to stay. That somehow, in the unpredictable way that the world works and how things are always meant to be, your goodbye opened new doors in this relationship that you both have not yet explored. However, life is not simple, and goodbyes are not easy. Especially when we say them to people who matter the most to us.

I also know that it hurts thinking about how you will get through the minutes, hours, weeks, months and even years after you say that one word but trust me – you will heal. Trust me, your goodbye to the person who makes you smile, but causes tears to flow out of your gentle eyes, will be good for you. You will feel hurt, yes. You will feel as though you gave too much importance to someone who did not think twice about you leaving – but it will get better.

Eventually, you will understand that the action you thought was the hardest to take has been the best thing that happened to you. Once more, you will welcome your worth which – in chasing them – you had long forgotten. You will come to terms with why they did not love you back and you will no longer care, because you will accept that everything happens for a reason. I know it hurts to say goodbye to people who matter the most to you but trust me when I say that with time, things get better and goodbyes get easier. Trust me when I say that it will all work out in the end and in your favour. Trust me, just trust me.

Love Stays

You need to remember that one day someone will come along, and it will make sense why everything happened the way that it did. It will all make sense. The heartbreaks, the lost friendships, the tears that soaked your pillow for weeks until the pain subsided. It will no longer be your throat, but your heart that skips a beat. And you will finally accept that true love makes you grow, not wither, true love makes you smile, not cry. True love fills your heart with so much happiness that there is no room for pain. And when there is pain, it is for them and not because of them.

One day, this person you dreamt of will come along and, instead of sweeping you off your feet, they will hold your hand and walk with you. It will happen, it must happen because you deserve all the happiness in the world and a love that makes you flourish. You deserve a love that teaches you how to love yourself, and a lover who will respect you and treat you as an equal. You deserve a lover who will respect you and never make you shed a single tear. One day, someone will walk into your life and they will not leave your side, and that is when you will understand that true love stays, it always stays.

And importantly, I have learned to do the one thing that most of us find so difficult to do – I have learned *to love myself* in ways that I never thought possible, and *this is what saved me.*

Your Growth

Trust me, it was never about the person who hurt you, or the one who let you go, or those who could not accept all that you were made of. Don't you see? It was always about you and your journey. They were just passers-by who entered your life for a short period of time. They were necessary lessons that you desperately needed. But they were not the important ones, because in the end – it was about you. It has always been about you. You were never broken after all, can't you see? Every person who turned away from you left a piece of themselves in your hands, and you used those pieces to change, to flourish and develop – pieces of them, you added to your own soul. They were the ones who lost – with no lessons to take and no hurt from a love that helps you flourish.

And in the end, they were the ones who cracked open because they could not mold themselves to make room for you. And when your light shone through their cracks – you grew, you grew.

Sadness

I feel sad. The kind of sad where your face heats up and you can feel tears brimming at the corners of your eyes, and the edges of your mouth start twitching because you really, really do not want to cry. Because crying is a sign of weakness and you are not weak, or so you tell yourself. I can also feel an ache in my chest where my sadness is clawing at my heart, because every time that I think of you – it falls. It is difficult to tell myself that everything will be okay, when it has been so long since things were. I do not know how to deal with this emptiness that the absence of you brings, but I know I must deal with it just like I did before, just like I always have.

But I feel sad. The kind of momentary pain that makes it seem like nothing will be the same again, now that I have lost you. But this pain will heal, so will the hollowness that arises when I learn that I can never speak to you again, and so will my feelings towards you. Time is the biggest healer and this, too, shall pass. But I feel sad, and I must tell myself that it is okay to simmer in my emotions for now, it is okay to let my tears flow.

Perfect Love

I have stopped chasing the idea of this 'perfect love' that will complete me. Instead, I chase the best version of myself. I chase self-love. I chase my pride and dignity. I chase my dreams. I have stopped looking up at the stars at night, in hope that they will sprinkle the magic required for wishes that I now know I can fulfil myself. I no longer need another person to allow me to see hope, as I see all the hope in my reflection in the mirror each morning when I grasp how long it took for my smile to finally feel like home. And I recognise how much I have endured to be here, to be present, and to be content.

I no longer chase people, or feelings or ideas of love when I have myself to come back to each night – and that is the biggest gift that I could receive. I can spend hours in my own presence and feel happy, and this is not there when I am with people who make me feel alone. I can give myself everything now. This is how I know that I am healing, that I am growing, and that I am putting my pieces back together to complete myself. Or maybe I already have – maybe I have reached that point where I am finally good enough for me. Maybe I have become the person that I deserve to spend the rest of my life with, and this is a relationship that I will keep forever.

There is *absolutely nothing wrong* with
love being soft and unspoken, and slow and steady.

Selfish

I must admit, we are extremely selfish sometimes. We are selfish because we keep people with incredible power over us close to us, not because we love them enough to get hurt by them, but because they make us happy. We keep these people close to us because we know that without them, our lives would be colourless. Often, we let them do things that pierce through our hearts like needles or treat us in ways that are unjustified. And it is not because they are generally unfair and wrong, but because we let them treat us like that, as telling them otherwise would risk them leaving us and that is something we cannot stand.

The reason why we act in this way is because sometimes our heart gets weak and turns greedy by gripping on to things that have the power to hurt it, as it knows just how happy those things make it. Our heart keeps everything that gives it life close to it, even if it comes with a little bit of discomfort. Our heart just wants to be loved, our heart needs that love and even if it turns out to be unrequited, our heart is willing to risk that just for a little bit of joy that love gives it. We can be extremely selfish sometimes when we listen to our hearts. Because, in the end, we will hold on to people that hurt us just because they make us happy, and that is the biggest paradox of our lives.

Time Heals

Time heals all wounds, and I know this as I sit here remembering you without a single tear shedding down my cheek. My heart has not known sadness for months, nor do I feel numb. Instead, these days I sing along to my favourite songs and smile whole-heartedly. I watch my favourite TV shows, and I read. I go out and have a good time and sometimes, when I look in hindsight at those dark dreary days when another minute felt unbearable, I feel grateful for the life I have been given. I feel grateful for a second chance to do it all over again. To live, to smile and to fall in love the way I was supposed to – with the right person this time, and a future planned together which would allow us both to grow.

Time heals all wounds, and I know this as I look back at the years that streamed by, with you as soft memories, and not the hard reality that I had to face afterwards. I am no longer broken, or hurt, or numb, or unsure about what I want. In fact – I am okay. I want to be happy and I want to live, and I want to keep smiling as I have been. I want this life. And I know this now more than ever as I sit here and think about how much I have yet to do, to achieve and to experience. Time heals everything. And the more I open my eyes, grateful for another day, the more I accept that this is the absolute truth.

Too Much Love

Let me tell you what it is like to love too much. Each morning, you get up hoping that you will not build a home in the wrong person this time, hoping that you will not give your heart to people who should learn to serve it. You hurt more than others, but you have become used to it by now, because you know that feeling this much is better than not feeling at all. You hand fragments of your soul to everyone you care for, in hope that they will cherish them, in hope that they will care in return.

And when they do not care, you crave for layers of yourself that you will never get back – leaving your soul half-empty, leaving you feeling alone. But still, your heart is too big and manages to forgive those who never valued you. And each day, you continue to spill love into the cracks of other people's hearts. Because you know just what it is like to not be loved in return, because you have been in the same place as them before.

You do not love me, and perhaps you never will.
But it is this 'perhaps' that I keep holding on to,
and that is why *unrequited love kills*.

Happiness

Sometimes, the only way you can achieve true happiness in your life is if you manifest it. The only way to get to the other side of darkness is if you send out the mental image of your happiness into the universe, as an idea, as a dream and accept that the laws of nature will work to ensure that you get it. The mental image of you doing what you love the most. The mental image of you living and breathing in happiness and spending time with people who fill you with affection. The image of you smiling with completeness, of you feeling content and at ease. Sometimes, the only way to become the best version of yourself is to manifest it as a beautiful idea and send that energy out into the world. Because the positive energy that you send out will eventually find its way back to you – the only thing you need to do is work hard and have faith that good things are coming your way.

Our experiences are nothing but a result of the energies we send out and receive, and our view of the world reflects the light with which we see it. So, have faith and accept that the only way to achieve happiness is to envision it and to strive towards it. And then watch how the universe works its magic to give you everything that you have ever wished for and have faith that even if it has not happened yet – one day it will.

Letting Go

We fall back on this fear of being left alone, of letting go of someone we love and never being able to love again, and of having our heart vacuumed of every emotion that we can feel the echo in our bones. It is not true. It is just a fear and nothing more, believe me. Once you move on from the things that break you, the people that hurt you and those who would easily let you go, your heart makes room for more. If you feel a void, it will not be for long – trust me. The hollowness will be consumed by a love that you deserve, and the coldness that seeped into your soul will be replaced by a warmth that will make you tingle.

Your smile will return, even if a little slowly, it will return. Just trust me. Letting fear take hold of you means still sleeping with tears in your eyes, still feeling a stabbing pain inside your chest, and still aching for the love of someone who is not worth your time. Letting go means accepting that something better is meant for you, it means appreciating your worth and moving on, it means having faith in life and the lessons you must learn. Letting go means choosing love over heartbreak, choosing comfort over pain, and choosing yourself over them.

Letting go means believing in yourself and loving yourself enough to walk away. Letting go means choosing your happiness over everything, because you know that you deserve it, and because you know that eventually – you will heal.

The Idea of Them

You do not love them, you just love the idea of them. Do you really know them? After having a few conversations with them, perhaps you think that both your minds are similar, perhaps your personalities are too. However, do you truly know them? Deciding that you are in love with someone after a handful of conversations about art, history, philosophy or culture is not a strong foundation for love. These conversations take you both on a journey as further away from reality as possible, and for love to exist – you must be in touch with reality. You must know as much about the real world as you can, you need to know about their world – to be precise. You must know the truth about the person whom you claim to be in love with, which intellectual or stimulating conversations cannot give you. Those conversations can tell you about their mind, but not their situation. Those conversations can give you a glimpse of their thoughts but not their feelings.

If you do not know about their life – their inconsistencies, insecurities, imperfections, burdens, struggles and the muggy reality that they live in, then you cannot know if you love them or the idea of them which was based on a few outings that were as detached from the real world as possible. This is the difference between love in the real world and fairy-tale love. Fairy-tale love creates a beautiful story, depicting a life of togetherness because of a few wonderful moments that you spend with someone. In fairy-tale love, you do not get to know their dark side and they do not get to know yours. In fairy-tale love, you have an image of them being the most near-perfect human whom you can spend a gorgeous life with. However, this is not reality. Real love happens after you truly get to know them, after you come to know their story, their darkness, their problems and everything messy and honest about their life that gives you an accurate account of how both your lives will be together. Real love is as practical as it is magical, and it comes after all the perfections have been stripped off from them and they are standing in front of you, their flaws laid out before you. So, before you decide whether you love someone or not, ask yourself this question – do you truly know the person whom you claim to love, or have you fallen in love with the idea of them?

Even after I had built a home in you, I felt like I had *no home* in which to live.

Pure Soul

No matter how hard you try to keep your heart safe, at least once in your life you will come across someone who will be like no other. You will watch them with kind eyes and an expression of disbelief at the possibility of people like them existing. A pure soul. The kind of person who only knows how to spread love, positivity and good vibes. They will come into your life like a blast of sunlight, making your heart fall for them recklessly. Madly. In ways it has never fallen before. And you will be happy, excited and extremely scared. Scared for your sanity, for the safety of your heart and for every dream you had about love that their existence validates.

No matter how hard you try to keep your heart safe, this person will come into your life and topple your world over in a way no one ever has before, and you will not even realize it.

Empty

I am empty. But I cannot feel it inside my chest because I do not feel much of anything these days. It is as though I have nothing to give to the world, and there was a time when I had so much within me to share – affection, goodness and love and, most of all, myself. But I have no idea who I am anymore. When I smile, I no longer feel the smile in my bones. I think my lips just curve upwards because I assume that this is how I should react at that point, but my reaction does not reflect what is going on inside me. Because the storm within me has become so calm that it will never rage again. And that scares me – this inability to feel things, to love and laugh and smile, and to be truly happy in the way that I was.

I have lost my soul, and I am scared that I will never find it again. And I do not know how to cope anymore. I know that this is just a phase in my life and soon enough I will be okay again. I have dealt with worse and I can deal with even more. But, how could I lose a huge part of me when I do not feel broken? How can I feel love again when I no longer feel anything? And how can I let happiness in when I cannot remember what it feels like to be truly happy? And this is what scares me the most.

Show Them Instead

Sometimes you meet someone, and you want to tell them everything about yourself. Your likes, your dislikes, your school experiences (including your favourite teachers and those whom you hated, your good friends whom you still speak to and those whom you have lost touch with), every small argument you have had with your siblings, as well as the tiny jokes that you share. You want to tell them who your favourite member of the family is and whose favourite person you are, and you want them to know the names of all your best friends – both new and old. You want to share your dreams with them and tell them how much you have changed over the years, you want them to know all the experiences you had as you grew up that made you the person that you are today, and you want them to realize how your feelings grew.

You also want to tell them the small things, like your pet peeves, your fears, your favourite ice cream and your favourite colour, the song that touches you every time you hear it and the book that made you cry, as well as your secret hideout and every adventure you hope of going on. You wish they could know every little thing about you too – the embarrassing moments and all your warm memories. And every big thing – the tears, the love, the friendships and all that this person has missed in your life when they were not there.

You have countless things to tell them and so much to share. But sometimes you fall short of words, and on those occasions, where you have so much to say and no words with which to say them – you wish that you could rip open your heart and show them instead.

I wish I understood it then, but now I know that
true love makes you grow, not wither.

Selfish Love

I wish that I loved you selfishly. Maybe then I would not hurt as much, maybe then my long nights would not drown me in puddles of restlessness, but in love. In the essence of it, and with the calmness that it brings. Maybe then I would sleep with a smile on my face rather than the ache in my chest, which does not leave me even when I dream. Maybe then I would not feel so defeated and damaged. I wish that I loved you selfishly. Maybe then I would not want to wipe your memories away but keep them locked inside my heart for safekeeping. Maybe then I would not keep convincing myself that it was not me who broke us, but you. Maybe then a whole lifetime away from you would be okay.

I wish that I loved you selfishly. Maybe then I would not have broken or fallen apart. Maybe then I would not be standing here and wishing that things were different. Maybe then I would be happier, I would be okay. I wish that I loved you selfishly. Because maybe then – I would have left and not you.

Another You

I know you have been made to feel like you are replaceable, or forgettable. You have questioned your worth because of this. You think that there is nothing unique about you because of the way one person treated you, and this is not true. You are unique in countless ways. Your personality, for one thing. Your quirks. The different smiles that you take to each day. Your strength. Your sensitivity. Your insecurities. Your kindness. Your imperfections. Everything that makes you the person that you are cannot be replaced or forgotten. Do not let someone else's treatment of you determine your worth. Do not let their actions define the person that you are.

You are a beautiful human who deserves love and respect and, more importantly, you are different in the best way. If you think otherwise then search the ends of the earth, look high and low, here and there, through every curve and edge and you will learn that another you cannot be found. Love yourself. Cherish your heart and forgive all those who fail to, for even they know in the deepest corners of their soul that they will never find another you.

My Past

My past was a teacher. But it taught me so much more than just whom to trust and whom not to, for I know that those are not the biggest life lessons. The past showed me the importance of being true to myself and seeking to become a better person. I learned about my flaws and my fears, about my inconsistences, my shortcomings, the things that held me back and those that brought me down. I learned that I, too, am imperfect and can make mistakes. I hurt others and fought. I screamed and shouted and said things that I did not mean. I cried for the wrong reasons. I was chaotic in my wake. There are several things that I wish I could change, but time has taught me to want to be better for my present, rather than wish to change my past.

My past was a healer, because after all those things, I learned when to trust myself and when not to.

You are not someone who loved my soul, because
if you did, *you would have cherished it*. If you
did, you would have cherished it – and that is
how I remember you these days.

Simmer in Love

On nights like this, I wonder whether this feeling of love will ever simmer. I do not know whether there will come a day when my heart does not explode at the sound of your voice, or when I do not smile this much as I think of you. But right now, you are the only person who makes me feel alive. You, being here, in my life as the brightest light that I have ever known. You are the only one who keeps me going. And I do not know what the future holds for us, and I do not know if you will ever feel the same way about me, and if you do not, I do not know how badly I will break.

But for now, I cannot let you go. Because you are the only one who gives me hope, even if there is no hope for us. You are the only one who makes me feel content without being anything other than yourself. You are the only one who makes me truly happy without knowing it. I do not know what will happen in the future, or how horribly things may end, but what I do know is that I will never find someone like you again. That is why I will remember every moment that I have with you now, and that is why I will keep you close for as long as I can. Because I need you, but I can assure you that you will never hear those words from me again.

Closure

Sometimes, you do not need closure. You tell yourself that you want closure, but the only reason why you want to speak to them is because you think that your 'final conversation' with them might change their mind. But you need to understand that in getting your closure, you are giving them respect, you are showing them that they are worthy enough to know the reasons behind your actions, and sometimes – they are just not worthy. The closure that you want, they do not deserve.

You need to ask yourself – will what I say to them make them a better person? Will it change the way they treat me or others in the future? Will they realize their mistakes? If your answer is no then your closure is a waste of yours and their time, because you have already made the decision to move on and, on this occasion, they have not earned the right to know. Remember, you do not owe anyone an explanation for your actions. However, if you still want closure to move on, you must do it for you and not for them. And you must accept that your closure will not change anything more than close old chapters. That is the only way that you should look at closure, because that is the only way that you will be able to move on for good.

And one day, the right person will sweep you off your feet. *Softly, gently, slowly,* and you will not even realize it.

Okay

I got there in the end. You know, that self-peace that I always wanted to feel after you. I got there in the end. Where, seeing you with someone else did not hurt, and waking up with no one to call my lover did not make me feel incomplete, and remembering you did not feel like the bitter after-taste of medicine. I looked back at the years that passed by after you broke me, and I no longer felt broken. And this was the journey that I wanted to take – to be where I am now. Where, I know that there will be good and bad days. Where, I will welcome some mornings with a grateful smile but on others, I will have to drag my feet off the bed just to face the world alone.

But I will be okay. Okay, after a childhood that forced me to grow up too soon. Okay, after hurtful friendships that threw me to my knees. Okay, after a love that broke my heart into a million pieces. Okay, after it all. Okay, because that is what I wanted to be all along.

Indifference

I do not look at you and feel pain anymore. Instead, I feel indifference. I am staring at a stranger, not someone that I shared so many years of friendship with. You can no longer give me warmth, because all you were able to give me was grief. And I do not hurt for you like I did before. There is no longer a human-sized hole inside my chest because it has been filled with so many things that I have felt since you. Like a sense of purpose, fulfilment, the love of my family and friends and gratitude. Gratefulness for the life that I have and the people that I love. Life healed the wounds that you gave me – and I am okay.

And even if you came back, you can no longer break me as there is no room for you anymore. That is why I am indifferent towards you and everything that you do because how do you look at your heart, a flourishing jewel inside your body that is giving you so much hope and fill it with something that once withered it away. There is no room for heartache or tears, because I cannot fill my soul with negativity when, for so long, it has only seen the positive. I do not look at you and see someone that I once loved, instead I see a stranger who taught me a world of lessons. I see a stranger who loved me enough to leave me in pieces. You are not someone who loved my soul, because if you did, you would have cherished it. If you did, you would have cherished it – and that is how I remember you these days.

I hope you finally accept that you are worth all the love that you give to others, and *so much more.*

Self-Discovery

Recently, I have gotten to know myself in the most incredible way. I listen to my thoughts, I go on long walks and I buy myself coffee. I read books and I smile to my reflection in the mirror. I say what I fear out loud, and I focus on the things that make me happy. I spend more time doing what stirs my soul than what causes it to crumble, and that is why I can say that I truly know myself now. I have grasped that all I really want is good company – someone who listens to me, shares my worldview and enjoys tranquil evenings spent alone. And I know now that the only person whom I should rely on to give this to me is myself.

I have managed to see the truth – that no one can understand me better than me. So, I continue to do the things that make me happy and, in the process, I continue to peel off layers of my soul – getting to know the real me and loving myself for it more and more every single day.

Give Up

When I gave up, it was never on love or the inability of others to return it. What I gave up on was this idea that the only thing that can keep me happy is love. I gave up romanticising love and I turned it back to myself – where it always belonged. I gave up hoping that someone would save my drowning soul and, instead, I relied on the sparkle of light that I found inside my heart – and I believed it. You see, giving up is not always a bad thing, especially if you are giving up on the negativity and on the things that can rip you open in ways you can never stitch together again. Especially if you are giving up on people who give you no reason to keep believing them, and on the thin thread of hope that maybe they will respect you some day. Especially if what you are giving up on does not fuel you anymore, nor does it heal you anymore.

Because when I gave up, I found myself in ways I never thought possible. And it was when I gave up that I was winning myself back all over again.

Some People

Some people leave your life, and that is it. They do not come back, and you do not get the apology that you wanted, and there is nothing more to the relationship that you shared beyond that moment. Sometimes people leave, not to come back but to make room for others who are yet to come into your life. And you must accept their departure as the end of everything between you two, even if you did not want things to end this way. Sometimes, one thing needs to end before another can begin. One chapter needs to close before you can start a new one. One friend needs to leave before another can enter. One heart needs to break before another can mend.

And that is the only way you can look at it without letting it break you.

And I still cannot understand it – if our pieces were not meant to meet, *then why did we?*

My Words

I have countless things to say these days. It is as though, the moment I sit down, my hands take a journey of their own and I end up writing for hours on end. Thoughts trickle out of me as if I were a fountain of poems, instead of a human with too many bottled up emotions. I do not know where all these words came from, but I am not complaining. Because I would rather have a heart brimming with a little bit of pain than a hollowness that screams my loneliness back at me. The stronger you get, the more alone you feel. But I would take this as a blessing, because it means that I do not need someone to save me, because it means that I do not need to have any expectations from others, because it means that my words are enough to soothe my soul with *it will get better*. Because it did get better, and so did I.

But still, I have countless things to say and not enough words to say them with. So, I will keep writing my lessons in hope that you will take the blessings, and I will keep walking forward in hope that you will walk with me, and I will keep healing in my journey in hope that we will heal together. Because I have too many things to say these days, and I am hoping that my words help you too.

Pain

Pain is tragically beautiful. Sometimes, it takes complete power over you. You sit at the edge of your bed and replay everything that has happened to you, wondering how your life turned out this way, and you can feel it clawing its way through your body and right into your chest, where it throbs inside your heart until it spills down your cheeks. Sometimes, it remains at the back of your mind like a song on repeat, evidence of all that you have experienced, often spilling out, often flowing inside you and preparing you for strength. Sometimes, it surprises you on a lonely night after a day well spent, a sharp reminder of the truth that you have not healed just yet, and there is a long path ahead of you that you must take before you are okay again.

On other days, it comes as a feeling of empathy for the person you used to be, who experienced the things that you did. On those instances, you are detached from whom you once were but still connected to that person somehow. On some days, those sunlit mornings dissolving into starry nights, it comes as a smile on your face and a slight sadness in your eyes to praise you. To show you that, despite it all, you made it. Despite it all, you survived. On those days, pain is nothing but a soft healer, the kind that commends you for your strength but also shows you that you are still human, and that occasionally it is okay to hurt at the memory of it all. The pain you feel on those occasions is not really pain anymore, it is a gentle reminder of all that you have experienced and how far you have come. And that, itself, is the biggest gift of all. It is the gift of pain that we all have the power to feel.

Toxic People

Good people can be toxic too. A person does not need to be bad, negative or mean for their presence to bring you discomfort. People who make us happy, shine light on us and care about us can also cause us the kind of pain that makes it difficult for us to continue having them in our lives. This does not mean that there is something wrong with them, or you, it just means that you both cannot mix together for too long. It means that you cannot have someone in your life if they bring you just as much grief as they do love. It means that this person is both good and bad for you, and that never works out, no matter who they are and what they mean to you.

And the sooner you accept this, the quicker you will be able to get rid of all the toxicity in your life – both good and bad – and the better able you will be in taking care of yourself.

Because if we could, we would move
mountains to make sure that you do not have
to climb them, *just to save you the pain.*
Believe me, we would.

Unrequited Love Kills

I am fed up of writing about unrequited love, but I have a human-sized lump inside my chest – constantly reminding me how difficult it is to look at the best thing that could have happened to you and tell yourself that it is okay to let go. I wish that I did not pour so much of myself into you, because now I feel like a bare shell with nothing to give, a glass that will always be half-full, because the other half of me has long since left. And I find it hard to accept that the most amazing person who entered my life and filled it with light, brought with them the kind of pain that I will spend a lifetime trying to forget.

How could this be? Where, an incredible human who teaches you to live again, ends up leaving countless pieces of themselves which you try and try to join with your own, but are unable to. Because if our pieces were not meant to meet, then why did we? It does not make sense. And I keep telling myself that you were nothing but a lesson, but deep down I know that you are the most beautiful blessing that I have received. And I am fed up of shouting into the void, hoping that you will hear me when I know that your hands are as tied as my own.

You do not love me, and perhaps you never will. But it is this 'perhaps' that I keep holding on to, and that is why unrequited love kills.

Understanding Me

I do not think people understand me. I mean, they 'get me' in the way you get what is happening on a TV show, or when a scene unfolds in a book. But to say that they understand me would be to allow them the benefit of knowing what goes on deep inside my heart, or mind, or both. And they do not. They do not know how I truly feel about people and situations, and they do not understand how I deal with stuff. And by that, I mean actually deal, not 'deal' in the sense of painting a smile on my face and saying, *'It is okay, I will get over it',* but the real kind of dealing. The one where I cry and cry until I have run out of tears and tissues with which to soak them. The one where I wake up in the morning but do not want to get up, the one where I smile and laugh and have the time of my life with the people that I love, but when I return home – an emptiness awaits me. The one that involves pages and pages of writing and healing and the need to move on, but the inability to. The one where I lose parts of myself each night and gain new parts each morning.

That kind of dealing. The one where I promise everyone that things will get better for them, but I do not believe it for myself. And the truth is, others cannot understand me in that way because I choose to forget it, or I pretend like it does not exist, because sometimes I wish that it did not. I wish I was not this strong or soft or able to cope, but at the same time so unable to cope with anything. And that is why when I say that others do not understand me in the deepest way – it is because every so often, I choose not to understand me too.

The Right Person

The right person will not come with a flashlight on top of their head, indicating that they are the one. They will not make you think that you are in love with them the moment that you lay your eyes on them. They are not going to sweep you off your feet in an instant. They will not cause you to feel something that you have never felt before, every second of the day. The right person will feel right in the comforting silence that you share with them. They will be kind, funny and safe. They will be your friend and your solace before they become anything else.

Yes, they will make you feel special and different, but in a realistic way. The right person will win your trust before they win your heart. Their importance in your life will be a gradual one. You will not be able to comprehend what they mean to you until you will ask yourself that question. And one day, they will sweep you off your feet. Softly, gently, slowly, and you will not even realize it.

I know that instead of pouring all my love into you, I must pour it into myself. That is why *I choose to walk away.* That is why I choose my heart over yours. That is why I choose comforting myself with my own arms rather than waiting for you to give me the love that will never come. And that is why – *I choose me and not you.*

Rise Once More

I wish that I could tell you the reason for your heart hurting whenever you think of them, or why they never showed up at your doorstep when they said they would. To fight for you. To prove that they wanted you in their life. I wish I could tell you the reason for every moment you have felt broken or every time you have felt fear. Fear for your sanity in the face of love and life and all the pain that it gave you. Fear for yourself and your inability to get back up again. I wish that I could tell you the reason for all those times God pulled you back from something that you wanted, or when he removed someone you loved from your life.

The truth is, I cannot give you reasons, and I cannot answer your questions but what I can tell you is this – each moment that broke you, made you. All those tears you shed, cleansed your heart of pain. Each broken piece joined together to create a new you. Someone stronger. Someone more powerful and fierce. So, no. I cannot give you a reason as to why you went through so much pain, but I can tell you the purpose. The purpose was always for you to grow, change, heal and become the best version of yourself. The purpose was for you to become the person that you are today. And that itself should keep you going. That itself should be reason for you to rise once more.

Goodbye (Part 2)

I guess this is where we say goodbye. Not the 'we might stumble upon each other in the future' or 'if it is meant to be, it will be' kind of goodbye, but the real one. The goodbye that says I am sorry it could not work out, but it is time to move on, I am sorry that we could not give each other the happiness that we deserved, and I am sorry that we broke each other to the point of no return. The goodbye that says there will be no 11:11 wishes, and no small buds of hope that linger at the back of our minds on lonely nights. The goodbye that tells us we were never meant to be, that this world had no place for us, or maybe it did, but we ruined it.

We broke something that could have been so beautiful, but there is no way we can change things now because it is too late. There is no way we can turn the car back around to where we only had love for each other, and there were no questions and insecurities and doubts, where there was nothing but love, and you, and me. At this point I have nothing other than goodbye to say to you, because my heart is fed up of playing games and I am sure yours is too. This goodbye does not open any new possibilities or reasons for us to be together, instead it closes old chapters and doors and every seed of hope that we had. And this is the point at which we say goodbye, because there is nothing left to say anymore.

Someone who *does not love you back* will never be able to appreciate all the reasons *why you sparkle*. This does not mean that they do not deserve you or you do not deserve them, it just means that you both *deserve different things*, and that is okay.

You Matter

I do not know how else to tell you that you matter. Your thoughts, your feelings, your dreams and ideas, your fears and anxieties – every little thing that brings you down and all those things which pull you up; they all matter. And you need to stop feeling that what you think is invalid, and that your experiences are not enough to justify your pain. They are, heck, they are more than enough to justify how you are feeling. And you need to grasp the truth that your pain does not even need a justification. The fact that you are hurt is enough to warrant the love and care that you need, so do not tell me that you are scared to speak with me, or him, or her about how you feel. Because as I told you – you matter in every single way.

I know that you refuse to believe it, especially when you question your self-worth. But you do matter. Every part of you is valid and everything that you want, you deserve, and listen to me clearly when I say that you are not alone in what you feel. And you most definitely will not be alone from hereon. You matter to me and everyone else who is in your life. Just take a step forward and tell us what you need. What can we do to help because, if we could, we would move mountains to make sure you do not have to climb them, just to save you the pain. Believe me, we would.

A New Beginning

Maybe our ending was not really an 'end', but a new beginning for both of us. A beginning that will lead us in the right direction, even if it is further away from each other. Maybe we needed to part ways because if we had not, then neither of us would have gotten what we truly deserved, and in staying in each other's lives, we were moving away from what our purpose was. And if destiny has chosen this for us, then we must accept that this is for the best, that perhaps this is what will bring light in both our lives and love will be able to fold into the cracks of our hearts in the way it would not have when we were with each other.

Maybe I was too soft for you, or maybe your hands were too hard to carry the softness that lay within me, and that is where we went wrong. And we must accept that sometimes things need to end before new beginnings can arise, sometimes people need to break so that they can truly heal, and sometimes love needs to leave before it can return in a different way. And perhaps that is why I will not call this an ending for us, but a new beginning, a new journey that we both must take, without complaints, without regrets and without bitterness for what could have been – and rather, with hope that life will bring us what we both deserve one day.

My Hope for You

I hope you do not spend another moment in your life afraid to make a positive change, one that makes your life better, even if initially it causes you pain. I hope you are not afraid to say what you feel, regardless of the consequences, and I hope you know that you will always feel lighter after your emotions spill, rather than stay in. I hope you realize now that friendships do not last a lifetime, but some friends leave an imprint on your heart for lifetimes to come. And that love does not break you as you always thought it did, instead it heals you and allows you to become stronger, kinder and more giving. Instead, love makes you happier, love fills your life with warmth and sunlight, love helps you grow.

I hope you accept that the love you knew before is nothing compared to love as you know it now. And that the experiences you had before were beautiful, but the ones you will have after today will be even better. I hope you look forward to the future and what it brings, and I hope you value your present. Your past is the greatest lesson of all, and I hope you embrace it with open arms as you would a lover – the kind who will only make you a better person, the kind who will push you to embrace your true worth, the kind who will always be a part of you, even after they leave.

I hope your tears become the soil from which your growth takes root, and I hope that you become the best version of yourself as time passes. I hope that you are in a good place in your healing journey, and if you are not, then I hope that you gain the strength to get there. I hope you took everything that you needed to from those who came and left, and I hope you were there for yourself throughout it all.

And I hope you finally accept that you are worth all the love that you give to others, and so much more.

I no longer look at you and see someone that
I once loved, instead – I see a stranger who
loved me enough to *leave me in pieces.*

Different Lovers

There will be those who love you recklessly. Their love will strip off your confidence, your warmth and your soft edges until there is nothing but regret and scars that will take a lifetime to heal. Their love will weaken you and damage your self-respect. They will make you question every positive idea about love that you had until you do not associate your dreams with love anymore, until all you associate with love is regret. There will be those who love you selflessly. Their love will make you smile and laugh, and their presence will always fill you with bliss. Life will feel like an adventure when they're by your side – and they will become one of your closest friends. Their love will have no limit, and they will always be there for you, even on days when you cannot be there for yourself. And you will try and try but your heart will not beat for them, and one day you will walk away from them so that they can find the love that they deserve.

There will be those that love you half-heartedly. Their love will only reach you in chunks of friendship and kind gestures but, for them, you will not be the one. You will give them your everything, in hope that they will feel the same way – but they will not. They will never go 'above and beyond' for you as they would for their lover, because for them you will just be a friend. And you will have to let them go, no matter how much you want them to stay because, this time – you will need to find the love that you deserve.

And then, there will be them. The one who will love you fiercely, but without any expectations. The one who will become your best friend, and your companion. The one who will make you laugh, smile and cry with joy and just by them being there, life will feel kind to you. They will feel like sunlight during spring, and they will show you how effortless love is. And you – you will love them back with your whole soul. You will breeze through life with their hand in yours, taking adventures and making memories, planning a future together and growing into the best version of yourself. And you will walk together with huge smiles on your faces and love burning in both your hearts, finally realising that this is what love is supposed to be.

Too Soft

I know you have been told that you are 'too soft' sometimes. You are too soft because you carry your heart on your sleeve for anyone who will show you a little bit of kindness. You are too soft because you give those who hurt you chances once, twice, three times and even four. You are too soft because you forgive too easily and too quickly. You are too soft because your heart aches when you see someone enduring even a tiny amount of pain. You are too soft because you will do things for those you love without questioning whether they would do the same for you. You are too soft because you love too much and too deeply. You are too soft because you let those you love, take you for granted time and time again. You are too soft because you let them break you, even though you never would.

But you are strong. You are strong because you go into the depths of despair and come out bolder and wiser than ever before. You are strong because you use your voice to empower yourself. You are strong because you helped yourself get back up again. You are strong because you wiped your own tears and you plastered your own wounds. You are strong because despite it all, you are still here, you are still smiling, and you are still healing. You are strong because you found yourself in so many ways throughout it all. You are strong because you have the power to love yourself, because you are here for yourself. You are strong because you will never give up on you, no matter who else does. I know you are soft, but that is not your weakness – it is your strength.

Because even after being soft, you are so strong, and is that not a wonderful thing?

Journey

I have nothing left in this heart. No words, no emotions, no complaints, no worries and no fear. Just a hollowness that crawls through to my bones. And it is weird to think that I do not feel anything, when at one point in my life – I felt more than I should have. I look inside myself and find all the answers to questions that I have spent so long carrying in my palms, hoping that someone would listen. And now that I have it all, the answers, the lack of pain and the company of myself, I do not know if I feel okay or just numb. I do not know if, after it all, I should feel this hollow. Because I am no longer broken, or hurt, or unsure about who I want, because I do not want anyone but myself anymore.

And it is this journey from loneliness to comfort that I need to make, to heal. It is this journey from nothingness to a heart filled with happiness that I need to complete. That is when I will have moved on forever. That is when I will have myself for sure.

Let me be the one. The one who can love you unconditionally, the one whom you can trust with all your pieces, the one who can show you just how magical you are to me – every single day for the rest of our lives.

What Love Does

One day you will learn that love does not hurt you or make you feel misunderstood. Love does not give you mixed signals or confuse you. Love is not one-sided or unsure about you, love is not one foot in and one foot out. Love does not lead you on to leave you or let you go. Love grips you by the hand and makes you stay. Love listens to your thoughts and understands you, love knows that you are not perfect, but it still accepts you – with all your jagged edges and scars. Love appreciates that you need time and it gives you space for your healing. Love does not make you feel unworthy, no, love teaches you that you are worth everything and more. Love does not hold you back or stop you from flying, love becomes the reason you spread your wings to touch the sky.

And the most important lesson of all – love teaches you new ways to love yourself, every single day.

The Next Time

The next time you tell yourself that you can never move on from them, the next time you feel like you will never be happy again – read this well. Remember the years that rolled by before you met them, the experiences you had and the friends you made. Remember the way the sun always shined a little too bright, and there was a softness in the air and life always felt okay. Remember the days you spent at school – the people you met and the teachers you loved. Remember your friends, the ones whose life you saved and the ones who saved you, remember the stories you shared in the corner of that old school library with the creaky door.

Remember the adventures you had – the late nights when you danced with your friends on the streets, the books you read, the movies you watched, and all those cold days you spent indoors with a coffee and your favourite movie. Remember the parties, the crushes, and the heartbreaks. Remember when you told yourself that, *'This time it feels too real'*, but you got back up again. Remember how your heart learned to heal. Remember the smiles, the laughter and the tears that drained your eyes.

Remember, that despite it all you continued living and you continued learning and you did not realize how life beautifully passed by. Remember the years that flowed effortlessly before you met this person. Remember every experience you had, the hurt and the happiness and how much you had to give. So, do not tell me that life will never be the same without them, because remember – you experienced life graciously before they came and, even if they leave, you will learn to live.

Forgiveness

Sometimes, the biggest gift you can give yourself is the gift of forgiveness. I know it is difficult to look at the person who hurt you and tell them, *'I forgive you for the pain you caused me'*, and often, we think that in forgiving other people we are letting them get away with what they did to us. But this is not true.

Forgive, because you are ready to take the next step in your life. Forgive, because you no longer want to carry the burden of their actions on your shoulders. Forgive, because your bones are heavy with the darkness that they left you in and you no longer want to move forward with it. Forgive, because you are finally ready to let light flood in between the pieces of your heart. I know that forgiveness can make them feel less guilty, as though they no longer need to be sorry for what they did to you. However, their journey is nothing to do with you anymore. Your forgiveness is to help you move forward without them, so whether your forgiveness allows them to be happy or indifferent – it should not bother you.

Forgive, but only for yourself. Forgive, because that is what you want to do, and do not think about anyone or anything while you are doing it.

And maybe I was *born in the wrong generation,* or maybe, just maybe, other people cannot understand love in the way that I do.

What You Owe

You do not owe people anything. You do not owe people an explanation for why you had to cancel on dinner – because you wanted to spend some time alone. You do not owe them a justification for why you ended up in tears when you were all having a good time and they assumed that you were happy, but no one knew that you were quietly dying on the inside. You do not owe people an apology for caring too much, or for always looking out for them, or for loving them too much and being worried about them. You do not owe people your time and effort, especially if they give none in return to you. You do not owe long-lost friends who once made you feel bad for who you were a, *'Let's meet up for old time's sake'*, just because you are no longer in the pit where they had left you. You do not owe ex-lovers late night conversations when they feel lonely, even though they claim to the world that they have moved on and are happier now. And you do not owe people your energy or your love, especially when you are the one who needs to heal.

Those who care about you will get that you need your time, and that you cannot come out because right now nothing feels good. Those who love you will know why you cancelled last minute, or why you ended up in tears on their special day, or why you no longer talk or smile or laugh as much as you used to.

Those who value you will get why you do the things that you do, they will accept that you are struggling to cope, and that you need your space but when you are ready you will reach out to them. Those who love you will not make you feel bad for changing during your healing journey, because they will recognise that sometimes things need to get worse before they get better. Those who love you will never question your love or care for them, because they will just know.

People who love you will always be there for you, even when they are not there in person – they will always be there in spirit. People who love you will know that they do not owe you anything and you do not owe them anything, instead – everything that you do for each other is out of mutual care and appreciation. People who love you will not make you feel bad about things that are out of your control, in fact, they will make you feel like everything you do for them is less because that is how much you want to do for them, rather than need to. Because that is how much you will love them, but they will never make you feel like you owe that love to them.

Up to You

No one else can heal you, they can only help make your pain bearable by listening to you, by giving you their shoulder to cry on and by trying to make you smile. No one else can fight the monsters in your head, or deal with your insecurities, or fulfil your dreams. Those dreams are yours to follow, those monsters are yours to chase away, and your insecurities are things that you must learn to accept and overcome. Others can only give you a helping hand, a smile and a few hours of silky comfort that helps you forget your worries for a while. But others cannot solve your problems, they cannot get a hammer and break down the walls of fear that you have built around yourself, they can only give you a shout from the other side to tell you that when you finally decide to break free, they will be there waiting for you.

No one else can mend your heart or put it back together, they can only pass you the glue of friendship and love, but it is up to you to repair your broken pieces. Others can only do as much as you allow them to, but in the end – no one else can save you, because it is up to you to free yourself. It is only up to you.

I wish I did not pour so much of myself into you,
because now I feel like *a bare shell* with
nothing to give, a glass that will always be half-
full, because the other half of me *left with you*.

Deserve Love

I am trying to come to terms with the fact that one day I will see you walking down the street with someone else's hand in yours. Happy, smiling, and with the glow of love on your face that I always wanted to bring. And I must accept that, one day, you will be in love with another – someone kind, caring and wonderful. Someone with a soft heart, a warm smile and a world of knowledge. Someone deserving of you. I am trying to accept that this is how life must be. Where, everything that I wanted to live with you will happen for you anyway – but with someone else. It is weird to think that you can have countless dreams with a person, hope for things and imagine a whole future with them only for them to live that future with someone who is not you.

I think that is the hardest lesson for anyone with self-esteem to learn. When you look at how happy the person you loved is with someone else who is gentle, sweet and deserves love, and then to look inside your heart and say, *'I deserve love too'*. Because deep down, I know that I do. I do.

The Bigger Questions

It is extremely difficult to understand that we can spend most of our lives hoping for someone to look at us with the kind of love that not everyone is lucky enough to receive. With the kind of love that shows you that they will do anything and everything in their power to make you happy. But when we get there, when we finally look into someone's eyes and see unconditional love and warmth reflected at us – we realize that we do not feel the same way. How can we crave love from another but when that love comes into our life, instead of melting us or making us shiver with happiness – it makes us feel awkward and nervous. We feel like something is wrong with us because we do not love them back. We feel selfish and guilty, because this person who tells us that they love us would do anything in the world for us, but we cannot find it within us to feel something for them. And I do not understand this.

I cannot comprehend how we can easily push away someone whose heart is filled with boundless love and care for us, and instead chase someone who would not give us the time of day. Why can we not love those who love us back? Why does it feel wrong to say yes to someone who loves us, but feels right to chase someone who does not care about us? Humans are difficult to make sense of. And more importantly, feelings are the most complicated entities that you could come across. You could spend so long loving someone and wanting them, and then find yourself falling out of love without knowing why. And you can look at someone whose eyes have love, and only love, for you and still be unable to return the same sentiment that they deserve.

It is extremely difficult to understand how we can spend most of our lives searching for the kind of love that we do not think twice about before pushing away.

In Awe

One day you will come across someone who will leave you completely in awe of them. Their kindness, their sincerity, their heart and the beautiful soul that you will get to know will leave you speechless. You will be shocked that people like this exist too. People whom you only read about in books. The kind of people who make you laugh and smile, making you regret that you did not meet them sooner. You will look at them and wonder how it was possible that someone else did not see what you see. How was it possible that someone else let this person go without digging in deeper to find a beautiful universe hidden within them? You will ask yourself how you got the opportunity to meet someone this amazing and those before you did not notice their light in the way that you do. Or perhaps they did, but they did not look any further.

One day when you come across someone like this, who is the definition of everything that you have been searching for, you will feel glad that those before you did not know what they were losing. Because you do. You do.

One day someone will walk into your life and, no
matter what, they will never leave your side. And
that is when you will realize that *true love stays*
– it always stays.

The Best Thing

I finally got over you. In the way you do when you have exhausted all your options and you no longer have a choice but to move on, otherwise you will be stuck in the same place forever. I picked myself up and held my heart in my palms – heavy, stronger than most – and I put it back where it belonged; inside my chest instead of by your feet, waiting for you to accept it. I looked at the pool of tears that fell from my cheeks and I promised myself that I will never cry again. And now my eyes are as dry as a desert where, even if I wanted to, I cannot cry for you. I do not feel anything for you anymore. No warmth, no sorrow, no pain, no hope, no expectations, nothing.

But do not assume that this is good on your part, because it isn't. Because when I look at myself, I feel sorry for you instead. I got over you because I needed to, but despite everything – you were the one who lost the best thing that could have happened to you.

One Day

One day, you will look up at the sky and breathe in the soft air and feel the warmth of life absorb you. You will no longer be concerned about what other people think or say, or who has conquered in life and who has not, or how much you have achieved compared to others. You will not keep counting what you do not have and start appreciating what you do have – like your family, your friends and the people who love and care about you. It will no longer be about searching for a love that will give your life purpose, but about sharing the kindness in your heart with others and letting the amount of love you already have melt your soul. You will not worry about the future or keep regretting the past – instead, you will live in the present.

One day, you will let yourself sway in the tide of life and collect memories as you would collect shells on the shore. And you will smile and laugh and dance, and you will stop searching for hope in external things because you will finally accept that all the hope, positivity and light resides within you. You will not fret, or worry, or feel anxious about things that you cannot control and instead, you will allow the laws of nature to take their course. One day, you will meet people, not with the expectation that they will be there forever, but with the hope that for as long as they stay in your life, they will allow you to flourish and grow and give you a lifetime of memories to remember them by. And you will not regret meeting them, even if they leave, or feel bad about getting attached too soon because you will accept that you are human and even though you know that nothing lasts forever, some people make you feel like you have lived forever in the short time that you have been with them. And one day, you will let your heart simmer in pain and you will accept it. You will realize that making mistakes, trusting the wrong people and unintentionally hurting others is all part of being human. You will learn that, in the journey of life, you are bound to get your heart broken and break a few hearts yourself, but you will not let that take away your love for yourself. And one day, you will finally get there. One day, it will all make sense.

Trust Again

I get it. It is kind of hard to believe new people when you have been broken once. It is kind of hard to love someone else when the one whom you loved, gave you no reason to love again. It is hard, but it is not impossible, and that is what you need to tell yourself. That when a new person comes in front of you, with a quiet twinkle in their eyes and a soft smile, ready to take your pain away – let them. People are not the same, and a love that broke you once will not break you again because the one who will be giving you that love will be different.

Just remember that experiences are there to teach us valuable lessons, and it is not loving that you should be afraid of – it is giving your love to the wrong person. That is what the lesson should be, and that is all that you should be taking from heartbreak.

I can tell you now that life healed the wounds that
you gave me – and *I am okay.*

I am Happy

To say that 'I am happy' and mean it is the most incredible feeling. I am happy in the way that matters the most. I am happy because I deserve to be. I am happy because I realized that my happiness comes from myself and no one else. I am happy because I look at how far I have come and how, at one point in my life, even existing for one more second caused physical discomfort inside my heart but now, after all these years, I feel strong in the face of a new day. I am happy that I lived through the darkest moments of my life and travelled far towards light. My happiness stems from appreciating everything; my journey, those highs and lows, the lessons, my family, the friends I have lost and gained, the soul-filled conversations I have had and how much I have grown.

And it is in these ways that we should understand happiness. Happiness is encompassed of all those things and more. When you say, 'I am happy', you declare that you have chosen light over darkness and comfort over pain. Despite the negative thoughts and those tiny monsters in your head, despite the long days and tough nights, despite the pain, the heartache and emptiness, despite the loneliness that you sometimes feel. Despite it all, you have chosen to feel a positive emotion at this moment. Despite everything, you have chosen to be happy right now. And that is the way in which we should accept happiness and that is the way in which we should appreciate it.

We Hurt Others Too

The problem is, we have spent so long being on the side that must leave to be remembered that sometimes we forget – other people can leave us too. And it is not always a good thing. Sometimes we lose people and then recognize their worth rather than it being the other way around. We forget that we have the potential to hurt those who love us, and to make mistakes, and to carry regret on our shoulders when it should have been left behind. We spend so long gripping onto the softness of our hearts that we forget how capable we are of turning other people's hearts to stone. We need to acknowledge that can we lose people who feel like warmth, and the kind of friends that take lifetimes to find. And we lose them, not because we are the victims but because we carried out certain actions that hurt them, or we did things that carved a distance so big that it can never be filled with tenderness again.

Sometimes, we are the ones who make the mistakes, who do the hurting and who cause the heartbreaks. And as much as it torments us to accept that we can cause the kind of hurt that we experience, and the kind of hurt that we blame others for, we need to accept it wholeheartedly to move on. Accept that you are flawed, and that you will hurt people in your journey, however long it may be. Accept that you may be the lesson that others need to learn, you may be the hurdle that they need to cross, and you may be the pain that they need to leave behind to be happy again. Accept the possibility that you may lose someone dear to you because you did not appreciate them when you should have, and when you will realize their worth – it will be too late. And accept that carrying the burden of regrets and the guilt of past mistakes will not do you any good. Instead, you must leave them behind and seek to do better.

And finally, accept that you may the reason why someone will stumble and fall and feel the cold inside their bones before they can stand up and be warm and rise again.

You Cannot Make Them Stay

You cannot make someone love you. A lesson that I have spent months trying to unlearn, because for some reason my heart and mind are still not on the same wavelength. It is simple, isn't it? Waiting for someone to love you back is like knocking on a door that will never open. It is like trying to build a life in someone else's home – but it was never yours to begin with. You are holding your heart in your palm and squeezing out all your emotions, just to prove to them that you are worthy. Just to show them that in picking you they will make the best decision of their life. As though you were a guarantor. As though someone needs proof to love you back. Love is not a game that you can win or lose because, if it were, loving someone who does not love you back is a game that you have already lost.

And no matter how hard you try to change their mind, you cannot. Because those who do not love you back do not know what makes you sparkle, they do not know why you are so special, and they will never be able to give you the love that you are worthy of. This does not mean that they do not deserve you or you do not deserve them. It just means that you deserve different people, and that is okay. This is something you must accept, rather than chase a love that was never yours to begin with. Because trust me, you cannot make someone love you, and no matter how you try, you cannot make them stay.

And maybe I have reached that point where *I am finally good enough for me.* Where I have become the person that I deserve to spend the rest of my life with. And this is a relationship that I will keep forever.

Self-Worth

You keep forgetting your self-worth and that is why you love the kind of people who do not treat you right. You keep forgetting that your heart needs to be cherished, not throttled all over, that your soul is a temple and your eyes deserve to shine, not cry. You keep forgetting how far you have come and how long it took you to move on from a past that broke you into a million pieces. You keep forgetting your journey and that is why you stumble into similar types of people – with attractive personalities and difficult hearts, with deep faces and shallow souls. People who may have never felt the same love that you have soaked your soul in, so what good could they be to you?

You need to remember the person you have become and how much you can offer this world, and then you will understand that you deserve someone who will offer all of that and so much more to you.

It is Not Okay

In life, how many times can you say, *'It is okay'*? It is okay if you say hello to me. It is okay if we start speaking every day. It is okay if we meet up for coffee. It is okay if we become friends. It is okay if you want to call me. It is okay if you start calling me every day. It is okay if we become best friends. It is okay if you start flirting with me. It is okay if you imply that you like me but do not say it. It is okay if you change your mind. It is okay if you tell me that we are *'Just friends and nothing more'*. It is okay if you continue to lead me on. It is okay if you say things that you know will hurt me. It is okay if the phone stops ringing. It is okay if we do not talk as much anymore. It is okay if you start speaking to someone else. It is okay if you break my heart. It is okay if you walk away.

But it really isn't. It is not okay, and I hope you realize that one day.

The Different Days

There will be days when the sun beats down too heavy on your soul, and all you will want to do is hide beneath the covers as the hours pass, until the light ends up reflecting the darkness that has settled inside you once more. Days when other people's smile will not be contagious, and you will not understand why they are happy, and you are not, and why the morning was beautiful for them but felt like a chore to get through for you, and you will reprimand yourself for being so negative and for feeling so low. There will be days when the emptiness will seep into your weary bones and you will feel lost, confused and alone, and nothing will make sense other than the tears that will pour relentlessly down your cheeks. There will be days when weeks will pass but you will not be able to get over the past, when months will fly by and you will not realize because the moment that your heart shattered will feel like just yesterday, and when memories of what was will follow you like darkness the size of a person, reminding you of everything that went wrong.

But there will also be days when you will pull back the blinds to let the sun in, where the light will fall on your smiling face and you will open the window to absorb the fresh air with your lungs. There will be days when you will go outside and join your neighbours' children in a football game, and you will make conversation with strangers on the bus and laugh with your colleagues and embrace your friends. There will be days when you will absorb life wholeheartedly, where you will smile and cry with joy and the love that you will find yourself falling into. There will be days when other people's presence will make you feel better, and your happiness will grow inside your heart and you will be grateful for life once more. There will be days when you will only feel pain and a void that cannot be filled, and there will be days where love will flow out of every curve of your existence. There will be good days and bad days, days when sadness crawls under your blanket and joins you for the night, and days when you are happy even in your sleep because of how blessed you feel. There will be all kinds of days that you take forward with you, the negative ones will break you down and the positive ones will give you love. And at the end it will be up to you, which ones you choose to live for.

All the care that I gave to others, I must direct it to myself. And all the love that I showered on others – *I must first spill into me.*

A Lesson

They are not coming back. And the sooner you accept this, the quicker you will be able to gather the broken pieces of your heart and move on. I know there is a part of you that wishes they realize what they lost, or that they reach out to you to make amends or apologise, or that they simply learn they should have appreciated you while you were in their life. But your healing should not be dependent on that, your worth should not be dependent on how badly they think they missed out after you leave. Until you do not accept that they are not coming back, you will not be able to truly move on. Repeat after me – *they are not coming back, and I need to learn to live without them.* They are not. They will not. And if, by the laws of nature that accord to a plan much bigger than us, they do – you should not be sitting there waiting for them. You must accept that some people leave because they are meant to, sometimes things do not go as you planned and, often you must walk on a path that you did not want to because that is what is right for you. The path that is sealed with heartache and filled with tears, with the hard reality of life as an open field in front of you, and a bucketload of memories left on the wide road behind.

And it is okay, because they were a lesson for you – the best lesson that you could have received. The lesson that teaches you not to glue your hopes to a single person, especially someone who did not know where to place you in their life, a lesson that teaches you that people are imperfect and bound to make mistakes, and that you must stop searching for dreams in them and start forming dreams of your own. Dreams that are only dependent on you to fulfil them. And it is usually the most difficult journeys that bless us with intense strength and the ability to become the best versions of ourselves. It is a lesson a lesson that teaches you about love – that you must stop counting the reasons why other people should be loved and start appreciating the many reasons why you are the one who is worth loving.

Hopeless Romantic

I am a hopeless romantic. I think that love can come in any shape or form. It can delve into your life and bring with it a blast of light that will leave you reeling. You will feel your heartbeat quicken in its wake, and you will lose the ability to breathe when it is near you. A love that melts your core and paints your world with happiness is the kind of love that I soak my thoughts in. But just as love can come unexpectedly, out of the blue and in the most wondrous way possible, love can leave as rapidly too. Soft in its wake, destructive in its departure.

But I am a hopeless romantic, I believe that love never leaves forever. After the hurt, the pain, the tears and every moment of confusion about its existence, love will always come back to you. Perhaps not from the same person, nor in the same moment, but it will surely return at some point in your life.

Tired

I am so tired of being strong. I am tired of saying *'It is okay'*, every time someone treats me badly. I am tired of being the bigger person and making excuses for other people time and time again. I am tired of constantly proving how much people mean to me when they will not do the same. It is difficult, isn't it? Having a big heart, having the ability to forgive so easily and so quickly, being the one that always tries their very best to make others happy. And still getting hurt, still getting taken for granted and being left behind, as though you did not mean anything.

That is the thing about being a good person. You give yourself countless excuses to look out for others that you forget to look out for yourself. And you keep giving and giving – parts of your heart, layers of your soul, sprinkles of your happiness and all your energy until you have nothing left to give anymore. And in the end, when they get everything that they wanted, and they start walking away without looking back in your direction, you are the one who is left with a hole inside your chest where your heart should have been.

It is this journey *from nothingness* to a heart
filled with happiness that I need to
complete. That is when I will have moved on
forever. That is when I will have myself for sure.

Since You

I have spent so long counting the days since you happened that I have stopped remembering the days that I lived without you. The late nights, the beautiful mornings when the sun shone so bright it hurt my eyes, the life-changing experiences, the adventures, the laughs and smiles and tears that fell down my cheeks before you. I kept saying that nothing will ever be the same now that you are not here, but I keep forgetting that nothing was the same before you came – it was different, but it was still beautiful. I lived a whole life before you just fine, and I keep forgetting that. And I must accept that even though nothing will remain the same now that you are gone, it will still be a great adventure and a learning experience for me. Even though things have changed and you dipped into my soul and found the shore but left me drowning, I know that there are new friends waiting for me, adventures I have yet to take, cities I have not yet discovered, food I am going to taste, stories that I will hear and experiences that I will have before I can say that I have lived a 'well-rounded' life.

And the truth is, I have not seen anything at all just yet. Some of my best days are still waiting for me, and I am hoping that I have left some of the worst behind. So, even though you came for a while and changed everything in a way I never imagined, so did those before you and yet I lived, and so will those after you and believe me, I will continue to live. And I have spent so long counting the days since you came into my life that I have forgotten the days that I have still got left and how much of my journey is still waiting for me. All I need to do is take a step forward. All I need to do is embrace life. Just like I always have every time someone walked away.

Let Me Stay

I wish that I could erase all your pain. I wish that I could solve your problems. You know, the ones crumbling your heart and keeping you up at night. The ones slowly taking away your smile and your positivity. The ones that make you feel as though you have the weight of the world on your shoulders. I know that I cannot fix anything, but what I can do is this. I can be the shoulder you rest your head on when your worries are too much to bear. I can give you my heart in which to pour all your pain so that you have nothing but love left within you. I can be your friend, your solace, the one who listens to everything you keep bottled in, the one who will not judge you, the one who will always care for you.

I know that I cannot fix what broke you, but just know this – I will always be there for you. So, let me stay with you while you heal, and just trust me.

Self-Love

6 things that I love about myself. I love my transparency. It makes me who I am because it means that I am unapologetically human – prone to making mistakes by trusting the wrong people with my feelings and secrets, but knowing when to accept it and move on. I love my sensitivity. My inability to detach myself from others shows just how much I care about people. I am wholly affected by things and I am not afraid to show it, and sometimes being sensitive means hurting more, feeling more and giving more than others. But it also means loving more and being loved in return, and I would not change that for anything. I love my strength. The fact that I have experienced more than my years show and did not let it keep me down for too long, tells me that if I have faith in myself – I can face anything. My strength allows me to heal and it helps me deal with the toughest situations, and that is what helps me grow.

I love that I carry my heart on my sleeve, not because I do not value it enough but because I feel that everyone deserves to have a piece. My heart has room for everyone, and in return it wants nothing but to be respected. I love that I am friendly and open with everyone, including strangers. Making conversation with people I do not know and learning about their lives gives me immense wisdom. It helps me understand that we all have a story to tell, we just need to pay enough attention to the tiny details.

Lastly, I love how capable I am of loving myself. Regardless of the dark days, of my lowest moods and moments when I feel broken – I still love myself.

Regardless of my mistakes and the lessons that I should have taken from them. Regardless of my regrets and every time that I let myself down – I still love myself. And that is something that I will continue to do. Regardless of how bad things get, I will continue to love myself.

And you need to accept that being happy today and hurting tomorrow *is okay*. Not feeling anything for the person who broke you at one point, and then feeling everything at another point *is okay*. Being confused about whom your heart belongs to, if it belongs to anyone at all, is okay. Hurting for people because of different reasons that even you do not understand *is okay*. Believe me, *it is okay*.
And *it will be okay*.

My Biggest Fear

My biggest fear is not living a life alone but being unable to look in the mirror. The only way this happens is if I treat myself with less respect than what I deserve, or if I let others do the same. Or if I constantly put myself down for being different. My biggest fear is believing other people's notions of how I should be rather than accepting myself in my entirety – with all my scars and jagged edges, with every emotion that I can trace on my bones, with every pain and regret and imperfection. My biggest fear is letting myself down by making decisions that are not good for me, decisions that could be avoided if I just learned to love myself. Like choosing other people over myself, or loving someone who does not treat me right, or waiting for people to come back when, if they wanted me in their life, they would not have left to begin with.

My biggest fear is spending my entire existence thinking about the 'what ifs'. What if they loved me back, but just needed time? What if I made the wrong decision by leaving? What if I said yes rather than no? What if I did not let them go? I need to accept that the 'what ifs' would not exist if there was a want, an inclination or a determinacy that we both feel equally for each other. The 'what ifs' would not be there if we had mutual connection. The 'what ifs' would not be there if we had love, and that is all. My biggest fear is stopping myself from taking risks and, rather, taking a stroll on the easy route, just because it is less painful. I need to understand that sometimes the paths filled with thorns and lined with hardship are the only way to reach your true destiny.

My biggest fear is living a life without adventures in countries where strangers become friends, and experiences with those friends turn into stories that you tell your grandchildren at 60. My biggest fear is letting life pass me by without absorbing friendship and the tenderness of love, and of never crying on someone else's shoulder or lending them mine. My biggest fear is not having enough kind memories to recall when I am grey and old. My biggest fear is merely existing, rather than choosing to live.

Answers

I wish I had all the answers. You know, the ones I am searching for when it is 2am and sleep is nowhere near, and I am staring up at the ceiling, hoping that my heart will find peace someday. You know, the ones I need when I am crawled up in a corner of my room with my back against the wall and my arms wrapped around me to keep me from falling apart. The ones I search for in every conversation, in every gaze, in every smile and every face since you. The answers that I know can only be found when I explore my own soul, after I peel off the walls I have built around my heart to protect it from no one other than myself. Because I have given it away too easily in the past, or too quickly, or to those who did not deserve it. The answers that I know I will find once I stop looking for them in others. Those answers.

I wish I had all the answers when I need them the most, because they always seem to come when I have changed and grown. They always seem to come when I do not know what to do with them. I wish I had all the answers. But they always seem to come when I am not asking those questions. They always seem to come when I do not need them anymore.

Do not bend over backwards for those who would
never mold themselves *to make room for you.*

The Day You Find Yourself

The day you find yourself will be the most incredible day of your life. You will stop relying on others to make you happy, your smile will come from within and you will not search for love in other people's eyes, because you will see it every time that you look in the mirror. The day you find yourself, you will wonder why you spent so many years walking on paths that resembled jungles of messed up feelings, where you found nothing but darkness, tears and heartache. But it will not affect you anymore, because you will have a hold of yourself in every way. You will have your emotions, your heart and your soul and you will not give it to anyone, because no one else will be able to take care of it the way you can.

You will finally realize that lovers are not meant to take you on a journey, but walk alongside you, they are not meant to fulfil you, but appreciate how complete you are in yourself. Lovers are not meant to break your heart each day, they are not meant to make you feel unworthy or unloved. The day you find yourself, you will realize how incredibly magnificent you are – imperfect, yes, but filled with so much goodness and light that you will strive to be even better each day. The day you find yourself will be the most beautiful experience for you, because after that, you will never accept less than what you deserve.

I Choose Me

I cannot express how difficult it has been. This, 'look at them as though they do not mean anything to you, even though your whole world is standing right in front of you' way that I am treating you. I know that there is no future for us. But tell me how to turn off these feelings that have filled my soul with so much warmth that all I ever do is buzz with happiness. This love and friendship towards you makes everything worthwhile, but I must pretend like I am not breaking inside. I must pretend that I do not miss you the moment that you walk away, or that my eyes do not ache to see your smiling face the moment that I hear your voice. I must pretend, I must pretend, I must pretend. And it is difficult to wrap my heart with the string of strength and self-love because apparently that is all I need, but sometimes, just sometimes, I want you to wrap your arms around me instead.

And it is so difficult to look at you and tell myself that, 'It is okay to walk away', when the truth is, I do not know if I will ever be okay again. But I know that instead of pouring all my love into you, I must pour it into myself. Instead of giving you all my attention and care, I must direct it to myself. And that is why I choose to walk away. That is why I choose my heart over yours. That is why I choose comforting myself with my own arms rather than waiting for you to give me a love that will never come. And that is why – I choose me, and not you.

You cannot make someone love you. And no matter how much you want to – *you cannot make them stay.*

True Love

I gave up on the idea of true love a long time ago. You see, when you are at your lowest point and the one person who promised you that they would be there for you no matter what, is not there – you learn a lot about 'love' in our generation. Because I always thought that love is about promises being kept and not broken, I always thought that love is about holding each other's hand, even if the walk is difficult to take. Because I always thought that being there for someone when they need you the most is all that relationships are. But I learned a lot. I learned that, often, people mistake physical attraction for love and when that fizzles out, so do their feelings. I learned that telling others what they want to hear just so you can get what you want from them is our generation's way of engaging in healthy relationships. I learned that most of us are 'all talk', because when it comes down to things getting real, the ones who told you that they have got your back are the first to jet out the back door.

So, I give up on the idea of finding true love, because I have realized that no one I have met can love like I do. And maybe I was born in the wrong generation, or maybe, just maybe, the others were not taught about relationships the way that I was and that is why they cannot understand love like I do.

The Power of Time

I told myself once that everything good takes time, but I do not know how much I believed it. I stepped forward into the light and tried to forget the darkness of my past experiences as much as I could, but deep down, really deep down, a bulge of that same darkness had made a home inside my heart and walked with me. It is a strange journey – the initial days of grief where you know that you need to move on, but the inability to. The constant self-talks that flutter from one end of your mind to the other, the reassurances passed to your reflection in the mirror, the fake smiles, followed by an 'I am okay, really', to your careful friends with worry in their eyes and empathy on their solemn faces. You take each step, as though you have shackles around your ankles, you look around, hoping to find someone struggling as much as you – the journey is always easier when there are two. But you do not find anyone other than the distant hum of your own heart telling you to keep going, to keep fighting – you are on your own on this one, but it is not meant to be a bad thing.

Then you see the light, a slight flicker at the end of the tunnel that resembles the halo of an angel, it is your saviour, your way through it all. It can be anything; a dream, a relationship, a goal, a challenge, a TV show or a book – anything that turns into your solace. And you grip on to the hope you find along the way, the friends, the lessons, the adventures, the tears and anguish, the happy smiles and sad departures that have joined you on your path to recovery. You told yourself once that everything good takes time and you did not known then whether you believed it, but now, looking back at everything that you have experienced – you are at peace with the truth. Everything good does take time, all you need to do is have faith and hope and stride towards what you want. All you need to do is believe.

Strength

Why must we learn to be strong? Why is it not a quality that we are naturally endowed with, a skill that is given to every person in this world? Because strength is a virtue that we must earn before we can use it. Think about it, we only appreciate the light because we know what darkness feels like. We know that darkness is scary and grim and uncomfortable in every way, and light is the opposite of all that. And that is why we accept the light and we choose it over darkness. That is why, when the sun is shining and not a cloud is in sight, we feel at ease, we feel calm. That is why when the clouds are dark, and it is pouring down with rain, and the sky is bleak, our feelings are overshadowed too.

We need to learn to be strong in the face of despair, because that is the only way we will appreciate the strength that can be found in our scars. That is the only way we will understand that overcoming our obstacles gives us the willpower to deal with so much more in life. That is the only way we will accept that strength is earned, not given, that strength is in being soft, not stone-hearted. That is the only way we will learn to serve our hearts when we are drowning, and we will learn to cherish our souls when we are alone. That is the only way we can understand that the strongest people are made from pieces that come from broken relationships or broken homes, from the direst situations and the darkest bends of life, from the need to stop the pain and from the courage that tells us to keep going on.

When I look at myself, I feel sorry for you instead. I got over you because I needed to, but despite everything – you were the one who lost *the best thing that could have happened to you.*

Do Not Settle

Do not settle for anything less than what you deserve. Do not give chances to those who have not given you a reason to trust them, and never think about 'what ifs' because there would be none if the one whom you loved, loved you back with just as much force. Give up on the wrong ones but never on yourself, and hope – for a life that is filled with so much light that darkness cannot be seen. Have the strength to fight for what you deserve and stop letting people treat you with love that is only half-complete. Stop searching for answers in other people, because the only signs that you should be following are the ones that belong to your own heart. Because when you choose to settle for a love that does not deserve you, you start to think that this is all there is and nothing more. When you start accepting love in small fragments that cannot fill the cracks inside your heart, you assume that it does not spread any further, and you start to believe that love always feels like this – half-full and leaving you incomplete. Because when someone does not love you as much as you love them, it hurts more than words can explain.

When you keep giving and giving and only get half of what you have given in return, you start to think that you are unworthy or unlovable. It is only when someone loves you with just as much passion that you finally learn - love never lets you think *'Is there more?'*. Love never lets you feel alone and love never stops you from loving yourself. Because the 'what ifs' do not exist when someone cares about you, the 'what ifs' do not make sense when there is friendship and communication, and love. Because there would be no 'what ifs' if your love was reciprocated, and you would not sit there, settled in a corner of your room by the tall window, thinking for the rest of your life about *'What could have been?'* Because it is only when you accept what you truly deserve and learn to fight for it that others start to see your worth too. And it is only when you listen closely to the voices of your heart that you take actions to protect it and do what is right for it.

Whom Your Heart Belongs To

In the end, it is the person you want to talk to after each exhausting day, the one you complain to and share small jokes with, even though you are both too drained to laugh wholeheartedly, the one who listens as you go on and on about how life is treating you, the one who makes you smile and cheers you up when you are feeling low. It is the person who wishes you good morning, the one who calls you in the evening to see if you are okay, it is the first person who comes to your mind when something goes right or wrong.

It is the person who understands your moods and deals with your anger, the one who knows that you are not perfect – but loves you anyway. The one whom you share everything with, the one whom you tell your fears to, whom you share your dreams with, the one who stands by you as you work hard towards all your goals. It is the person who respects you for who you are and does not try to change you in any way – that is whom your heart belongs to.

Do not crack your heart open for those who would never *spill love* into it.

Over Here

One day you will learn to make peace with your past. Thinking about what happened might cause you discomfort but it will no longer cause you pain. You will come so far from what happened and who you were that a part of you will cherish the lessons you learnt along the way. Perhaps you will even be grateful for the experience because of what it taught you and how much it allowed you to grow. One day, you will reach a point where your heart will no longer hurt, and each painful experience will be a distant memory, fading far away into the past. And you will think about the present and be grateful for a future.

Over here, you will find countless reasons to love and to live. Over here, you will find peace and contentment. Over here, you will find the seeds to your happiness and a route towards your dreams. And over here – you will finally find yourself.

Alone

I am tired of writing about pain. I am tired of writing about love bringing with it nothing but heartache because that is not true. Love is beautiful – when it is felt for the right person, when it is returned and when it is experienced with your best friend. Love really is beautiful. But why do I always experience the side that hurts? The side that only causes an ache inside my chest, the side that is felt for the wrong person or is never returned, and the side that wants to be experienced, but never will be. The words that I use to describe love will always resemble an emptiness in my bones that no amount of writing can fill, that no amount of poetry can heal.

Unrequited love/ painful love/ a love that is felt for the wrong person – all feel like a poem sent out as a cry into the world which no one can hear. And I am tired of writing about a love that is never my own, but if the pain is what keeps me writing, then I guess I will be walking on this path alone.

Underrated love

People often say, *'Love is overrated'*, but I do not understand this. If we categorise it romantically, then perhaps it is, but we cannot forget the many ways in which love moves us. You love your parents, your siblings, your aunts and uncles, your grandparents, your friends, and your teachers. Love moves you to bite your tongue rather than hurt someone with your words, love moves you to be nice to strangers, love moves you to give charity, love moves you to help others. Love moves you to be kind. Love moves you to be there for your friend when they need someone to talk to and pat them on their back or offer them your shoulder to rest their head on. Love moves you to wish well for others, love moves you to pray for children suffering in war-torn countries and help those who are in need.

Love moves you to take care of yourself – both physically and emotionally. Love moves you to carry every good action in your life and spread light to those around you. But then I hear you say, *'Love is overrated'*, as if that were the truth. As if love is not the most underrated emotion, as if love is not lacking in most actions that cause pain. Love is not overrated. It is the most important sentiment that acts as a force behind every kind action – spreading positivity and bringing happiness. And love is the one sentiment lacking in actions that come from a place of unkindness, especially in places where there is only darkness and suffering. Love is the most underrated emotion in the world, an emotion that has become lost in the chaos and the egoistic race to success.

And that is why the world has become this way.

When you stop giving people parts of yourself, losing them no longer means that you *are losing you.*

Succession of Moments

A few days ago, I thought that I would never feel okay again, but today – I am feeling better. I smiled for the first time in weeks and I meant it. Dark thoughts were no longer running around in my mind, and I was not feeling negative or lost or completely incapable. In fact, I felt okay. And this made me realize a lot. Like how healing is not always straightforward, but it is definitely a journey – one that takes you through so many bends and curves of life that you almost feel like you will never make it, but somehow you do. Because today, I can sense it. I kept thinking at the back of my mind that this time I would not make it, that I was exhausted of energy, that I was out of willpower, and that this was it – this was the end of me. I also woke up not feeling any different, it was just another day filled with the same numbness.

But suddenly, I smiled. It was a short, brief smile, but it was enough to indicate that I was having a good time. It was enough to indicate that I had not lost my sense of happiness. I guess what I am trying to say is that there is not a fixed point at which you 'see the light' or 'come out the other side', there are just a succession of moments where – in hindsight – you see yourself getting stronger and better and happier. And often we clasp on to the negativity to such an extent that we think the positivity has faded away, even when something good happens, we try hard to remember the bad because we think that something is wrong with us if we no longer think about it.

However, we need to tell ourselves that it is okay. We are on a journey and the journey is slow, but one that we will eventually get through. We will learn and heal and grow and be ourselves again – we just need to give ourselves time.

Dear Self (Part I)

Dear self, thank you for the way you held on this previous year – it has been a tough one. You had some of the most incredible experiences of your life, but you also felt pain like never before. You loved, gained and conquered, but you also lost, fell and were scarred in countless ways. But you remained strong. You pulled yourself up time and time again. You did not stay negative for too long or let yourself churn in sorrow. You smiled once more, and you kept those who made you happy close to your heart. You danced and cried with laughter, you loved like you have never before, and you also got hurt in new ways. But you knew how to deal with the pain this time, you knew because you have been through it once and nothing can break you as much as the first time. You wrapped yourself with your own arms when you felt cold and you wiped your own tears, and you did not let yourself feel alone.

And I am so proud of you. I am proud of your willpower, of your strength and of your ability to deal with pain. I am proud that even after losing parts of yourself, you have added new parts and uncovered your soul with dedication. Even after feeling bare, you have become more whole and complete as a person, and I love you for that. I love you for holding tight and for taking care of yourself. I love you for not losing hope. And I love you for believing in happiness and for giving yourself everything that you deserve, and lastly, I love you for being relentlessly brave, despite it all.

In the end, we will hold on to *people that hurt us* just because they *make us happy*, and that is the biggest paradox of our lives.

Just Me

I am not here to prove myself to you. Where somehow, I will say everything that you want to hear and act in a way that tells you that I am the one. No. I am going to be myself. I will care about you because you deserve it, because you are worthy of my friendship and love and attention. I will give you the respect that you give me because your heart is pure, and your eyes kind and you do not know any other way to treat people other than with warmth. I will be your best friend. The one whom you can tell all your secrets. Even the deep dark ones that you keep hidden because you are afraid that if anyone finds out what is inside you then either they will be surprised, or shocked, or even scared of how much you have kept hidden in your heart. But I will not. I will understand because I get it. I will be all that I can be, because it is in my heart to treat you with kindness and sincerity and a lot of love. Because it is within me to give you every ounce of warmth in my soul, as I do not know any other way to treat someone whom I love and care about this much. As a friend. As a best friend. As family.

I am not here to prove myself to you. Where somehow, I will say everything that you want to hear and act in a way that tells you that I am the one. No. I am going to be myself. The only way that I am meant to be. The only way that you should accept me. And if it turns out that the person that I am somehow coincides with the person that you are, and we fit like missing pieces of a puzzle, then I will accept it and maybe you will too. But I will not try to be something that I am not. I will just be me, and I hope that you will just be you too.

My Place in the World

I guess I am still trying to figure out where I belong. I am trying to come to terms with my place in the world. You see, sometimes I know exactly what I am here to do. Sometimes, I wake up in the morning and my eyes are fierce with the light that I wish to spread to the lives of people everywhere. But sometimes, those long tedious days when the sky is grey and the sunlight dim, I lose track of what I am doing. I forget my purpose and my goals, and I want nothing other than to curl up under a rock. I want to forget everything and everyone for a while and tuck away into the tenderness of my heart.

We are all on a journey. We are all trying to unravel the meaning of life while staying open to new possibilities with each new day. We are making small attempts to welcome our growth and learning experience, but sometimes we are still lost. Sometimes, we worry whether we will ever know what we are here to do. Sometimes, we search frantically in the eyes and arms of others for a sense of meaning that we cannot find within the folds of our own souls. I guess what I am trying to say is that life is a gentle but raw journey, and sometimes, the struggle is real. But sometimes, the lessons and the wandering are not as rough on our spirits. Sometimes, we realize that we will get where we are supposed to be eventually – because that is the only way we can truly heal and grow.

Love Myself

Yesterday, I sat down and re-read the goodbye poem that I had written you. I felt liberated. I cried a little when I read it but a part of me felt lighter, because I have not cried for you since we stopped speaking and I was starting to feel like I am losing the ability to feel anything. So, it is nice to cry sometimes. It is nice to think about you, and your smile, and your laughter, and your humour, and cry. It is nice to accept that some people can cause you a lot of pain but also give you unbounded happiness. Because you did that for me. You made me appreciate my worth and welcome my dreams in a better way. You made me smile and laugh and absorb life in all its shades. You allowed me to uncover parts of myself that I had lost long before you, and it has been nice to find me again. That is how capable you were – you are – of changing me. For good. For better. For myself.

So, it is nice to see all that in hindsight and cry. Because I lost you, but it is nice to finally accept that it took losing you for me to love myself all over again.

Our experiences are nothing but a result of the energies we send out and receive, and our view of the world reflects *the light with which we see it.*

Grief

Grief does not always cause an ache inside your chest. Sometimes it is an emptiness, a numbness that crawls through you like the blood in your veins and settles deep inside your heart. Sometimes grief is nothingness – an inability to understand what is going on, an inability to emote, or empathise, or speak about things. Sometimes grief is sitting on the side-line and watching each day trail by. Sometimes, grief is the inability to move on, it is the inability to not only tell yourself that you will be okay but also believe it. Sometimes, just sometimes, grief is feeling so lost in the world that you cannot comprehend how to go on, that you cannot understand how to cope anymore.

That is when grief does not hurt but pulls at your soul the most – that is the kind of grief that can kill.

The Most Amazing Thing

Do you know what is amazing? When you open your eyes in the morning with a gentle smile on your face and a warmth in your heart that tells you how at ease you are. When you no longer compare yourself to others, and you no longer think that you are too fat or too skinny, or too fair or too dark, or too much or not enough. When you stop counting your imperfections and start counting your blessings – the blessing of having a kind heart and a strong soul, the blessing of feeling a lot more than others, because you use it to help more than to hurt, the blessing of loving too much and too quickly because it makes you feel alive. Do you know what is amazing? When you stop looking at your shortcomings as embarrassments and start embracing them, because they are a part of you and they are what makes you beautiful. When you look back at every mistake and stop reprimanding yourself for it, and rather, you accept that you are only human, and things are bound to go wrong.

Do you know what is amazing? When you finally look in the mirror and tell yourself, *'I am so proud of how far I have come, and I have a long beautiful journey ahead'*. When you get to a point where you have nothing but good wishes for those who hurt you in the past or did you wrong, because you are a kind-hearted person and you see this as a blessing rather than a curse. When all you want to do is spend time alone because that is when you feel the most content and at peace. And the most amazing thing is when you keep coming through from painful experiences, even stronger than before, because it shows how far you have come and just how much you have grown.

A Second Chance

There is no such thing as giving someone a 'second chance' when they come back. They must earn a second chance. They must show you that they will not repeat their previous mistakes, that they will cherish your heart this time round and they will not hurt you in the way that they did before. They should gain your trust, and if that means starting all over again by being friends, then so be it. If that means taking a few steps back and keeping one foot in and one foot out, then that is also fine. Remember, the burden of proving that they will not hurt you is on them, not you. And if they hurt you one more time – then you must walk away.

Do not give someone a second chance, as though your heart is something that you carry on your sleeve, valuable enough only to hand out for free to anyone who asks for it. Let them work hard for a second chance, only then will they be able to see just what your heart is worth. Only then will they be able to see just what your love is worth.

Letting go means choosing your happiness over
everything, because you know that you deserve it,
and because you know that eventually
– *you will heal.*

I Did Not Love You

I do not know what to say anymore. I did not love you, but it would not have been hard to. And now, a year and a half, hundreds of conversations and churned emotions later – I miss you. I gave you the best parts of me, parts that I will never be able to replace, and that is what hurts me the most. You took my essence without realising it. You changed my life without a clue. And you taught me what it means to love without loving me at all. And the 'what ifs' will haunt me forever. What if we had given each other a chance to be more than friends? What if we spent more time together, would things have changed? And most of all, what if we had fallen in love?

And I have no way to answer these questions without feeling my stomach descend like a packed elevator. Because you never spoke enough, and sometimes – I spoke too much. So, I keep the questions to myself with no hope of answering them, and I let you let me go, because that is the only 'what if' we managed to answer.

What if he does not let me leave? But you did. You did.

A Happy Life

A happy life does not consist of just happy moments, it is a mixture of both the happy and the sad. There will be good times – when you laugh with your friends until your cheeks are red and your stomach hurts, and the trips to the park and the zoo, and the shopping and the late-night ice-cream runs, and the private jokes and the notes passed in class, and every little prank that you play. There will be long lazy days spent at the beach where you dip into the ocean just as the sun sets, and the holidays to countries with tender sand and a warmth in the air, and the nights you spend indoors with your family wrapped around you, and the comforting days that you spend alone.

There will also be bad times – when your heart breaks in two and only your tears can fill the cracks, when nights pass but the pain will not pass, and even when the days shine bright, the light will not be able to pierce through the darkness that has made a home inside you. There will be fights, and hurt, and pain, and regrets that you wish you never had, memories you wish you could erase, and fear for what the future holds. There will be broken relationships and a lot of sorrow, but there will also be endless smiles and happy cries. A happy life consists of both feelings of joy and sadness, of love and pain, it is a mixture of both the light and dark, of a little bit of sunshine and lots of rain.

The Fear of Loving Again

Often, the fear of being hurt again is what stops us from giving new people a chance and from stepping out into the unfamiliarity of love and relationships once more, while knowing how much pain they can cause. It is difficult, it is so unbelievably difficult. And I know. I know that trusting someone new feels like standing at the edge of a mountain and hoping that you will fly rather than fall. Because you have trusted people in the past and they have let you down more than once. That is why handing over your heart to someone who wants you to trust them feels messy, and terrifying, and exhausting. But it is up to you to give happiness another chance – it is completely up to you. Love is chaotic, and I cannot guarantee that you will not get hurt again – but believe me when I tell you that love is worth it. You cannot keep your heart caged forever for fear that it might break once more.

Broken things can be fixed, even if they are not the same as before, even if the fractures shimmer through and all your scars can be seen, believe me – love can pour into them and give your soul a reason to smile again. I know that it is hard to trust new people, and I am not telling you to unless you are ready for it. But if fear is what is stopping you – do not let it. Especially if you want to let love in, especially if you want to be happy again, especially if you are ready to take a new step in your life, and especially if you believe that each one of your broken pieces form a step towards something that is truly meant to be for you.

I wish that *I loved you selfishly.* Maybe then, I
would have left and not you.

Best Friend

Have you ever looked at your best friend and wondered how badly it will hurt when they fall for someone else? Have you ever thought about how much it will kill you to see them loving and caring for someone else? And you know the person whom they choose will be extremely lucky because they will get your best friend as a life partner. Your best friend, who is this bundle of joy and happiness and a soul filled with so much love. You know just how lucky their partner will be because you have been so lucky to have your best friend in your life until now. Have you ever looked at your best friend and wondered about the pain you will feel when they finally tell you that they have found the love of their life, the love that you sometimes – in the tiniest, smallest, most secretive corner of your heart – wished was you.

But you chose not to tell them because you did not want to break your friendship, because having them in your life was much better than telling them how you feel and losing them forever, because you knew that they would never feel the same way about you. Because you knew that for them you are just a friend and nothing more. So, you kept your feelings to yourself and you buried them so deep that even you forgot that you felt a certain way about them. But have you ever looked at your best friend and wondered how badly your heart is going to break when they leave you? Because it will, believe me, and deep down you know that when the time comes, there will be nothing you can do about it.

Tender Hearts

It is not true when they say that tender hearts break easier or quicker. They do not. Tender hearts are softer and gentler, tender hearts are kinder and warmer and friendlier, and that is what makes them special. Tender hearts do not break but mold themselves to make room for others. Tender hearts shift and shape and absorb the hurt as well as the affection that those they care about give them, they do not crack – instead they adapt to change, they even hurt and become a little scared to trust new people again, but they continue to grow. You see, people with the tenderest hearts love more, care more and feel a lot more, but they are also the strongest. People with tender hearts can experience a lot more sorrow than those who do not know how to adjust themselves to pain or negative experiences. People with the tenderest hearts are sensitive to the wounds that others carry on their backs, they understand, they accept, and they learn from their experiences to help those around them.

For too long I have felt like my tender heart gets me in trouble with love and heartache, but I have finally realized that it is this heart that has kept me going for so long. It is this heart that allows me to witness the discomfort of half-fulfilled promises and a love that is never 'truly there' and still love, still give and still care about those in my life. Tender hearts do not hold grudges or toxicity, instead, they sprinkle light and magic in the lives of all those whom they meet.

A New Love

For years I thought that love only happens once and after your heart breaks, your capacity to love another person diminishes. I was completely wrong. It is not our ability to love that dies but our faith in love's ability to remain in our lives. I am not saying that you can love with the same force as you did the first time, but I am not saying that you cannot either. Love is not bound by the contingency of our experiences. Love is free. Love is boundless. Love is infinite. Love is open air and gravity at the same time. Love is the wind that sweeps you off your feet and the ground that balances you. And our capacity to love continues, even if our faith in love does not.

So, of course you can love again. But do not expect it to be the same kind of love. Do not expect yourself to delve in deep and trust someone new with all your heart the moment that you meet them. Do not expect this love to give you crazy jitters or fantasies that keep you wide awake at night straight away, or always. Do not expect childish murmurs of your heart and a gentle hum of your soul at the sound of their voice. It will come slowly. It will arrive when it is supposed to. Expect happiness. Expect a friendship that will bring you sunlight and shower you with the kind of rain that brings wide rainbows with it. Expect loyalty. Expect trust. Expect a new adventure on this journey that you decide to take.

And do not be worried that this emotion is different to what you have known love to be. Because it is still love in every sense, but it is a different kind of love. It is a new love.

Wait and watch how the universe works its magic to give you everything that you've ever wished for and have faith that even if it has not happened yet – *one day it will.*

Counting Stars

You must be tired of counting stars and hoping that one of them falls, just so you can believe that there is beauty in chaos, just so you, too, can feel beautiful for once. You must be tired of how easy it is for people to stream in and out of your life, as though you were nothing but a piece of art on display, waiting to be misinterpreted, waiting to be left behind. You must be tired of how quickly love turns a shade darker and feels heavier on your bones, and while you find yourself wondering how things became this way, it disappears into thin air once again. You must be tired of constantly being made to feel like you are not enough, like you are beautiful, but only from afar, like you are longed for, but only from afar. Because the moment they come close enough to see your imperfections and scars – they no longer like what they see.

Suddenly you become too little, or not enough, or too much for them. Suddenly you become a dream that they wanted to achieve, but now that they are here, it is no longer as magical as it seemed. Suddenly you are the prize and now that they have it, they want to lock you up in a small glass cage. Because suddenly their love is not vast enough to fill the well of your heart anymore. Suddenly they do not know how to love you for you anymore. Suddenly it is not them and you fighting the world together anymore. You must be tired of telling yourself each day that you are worthy of love, happiness and all your dreams when, every person you have ever wanted has made you feel otherwise. When every time you have felt love, it has not been returned with just as much force. You must be tired. You must be tired of how quickly magical moments turn into wishes that you can trace back to a time that was much happier than this. You must be tired of how easy it is for people to love you and let you go, for people to love you and hurt you, for people to love you and break you, for people to love you and leave you behind. You must be tired, my love, you must be tired.

When the Time is Right

Listen to me – things do not get better straight away, they take time. Moving on from hurtful experiences can take days, weeks, months and even years. But that does not mean that you will not eventually reach the peak of calmness – where you always wanted to be. Give yourself space and as much time as your heart needs. Healing is messy, and life is like a long school day – where you acquire new information, continue to have experiences, take lessons and absorb different kinds of sadness and joy with you as you propel forward. And sometimes you feel heavy, as though you have shackles around your ankles and a boulder of regrets on your shoulders. And sometimes, your soul feels gentle and your heart beats like a soft breeze. But you do not get better instantly, especially when you experience heartbreak, lose friends or live in a broken home. Especially when you experience the kind of grief where you empty out the contents of all your life's happiness into an ocean of despair and do not know how to come out from it.

Things take time and believe me when I say that this time could be anywhere between weeks to years – so, please be delicate with yourself. This journey will get easier, but not straight away. Be patient, and calm, and do not beat yourself up about getting upset over things that you feel you should have gotten over years ago. Every person's journey is different, and this is yours – this falling, breaking and healing, this hurting and crying and learning to smile again. You will get to where you are meant to be one day but remember – you always get the happiness that you deserve when you are meant to. Not when it is too early and not when it is too late, only when the time is right.

And in the end, it is the person who *loves you for who you are* and does not try to change you in any way – that is whom your heart belongs to.

Walk Away

What must you do when someone is not ready to be with you?

You walk away. Love yourself enough to walk away from anyone who does not know your worth. Believe me, one day you will meet someone who will drink up every ounce of your magnificence, making you wonder what you were doing wasting your time with someone who had no idea what you truly deserved. Walk away from anyone who is unsure about you, no matter how right you think it feels. Because at the end of it, if they were so right for you then you would not be losing sleep over why you both are not together.

Karma

It is no longer about wishing that 'karma gets you back' for what you did to me. It is about praying for your wellbeing, your good health and your happiness. It is about hoping that one day you stop drifting and find a home in someone else's heart, and that you find the kind of love you would not with me, because that is what led you to do what you did. That is what causes you to act this way – with a craziness in your eyes as you search for meaning, hoping that you will find it somewhere, but the moment you cannot, your face shuts down and your eyes lose their thirst. It is about wishing that your experiences help you grow and become someone that another would be lucky to have. It is about longing to see you succeed. It is about wanting your betterment. It is about wishing that you have a lifetime of love without pain. It is about hoping to see you smile, no matter what you did to me, whenever I see you next.

That is what love is. That is what love is about.

Be this Person

Be the person who breathes in self-love and breathes out their insecurities. But do not think that if you have insecurities then there is something wrong with you. Do not think that being confused, unsure or feeling imperfect means that you are less than others. Do not believe that your anxiety makes you a lesser person, or that the gradual darkness that you find creeping into your mind is all that you can give to the world. Do not feel that you are weak or incapable just because you re-think your dreams, or you do not know what path to take to achieve your goals. Do not think that you do not have any ambitions, just because you do not have a set plan. Accept the spontaneity of life. Accept the uncertain course that life takes and the possibility that there will be countless ups and downs, and you may take several detours before you reach your destination. Accept the idea of leaving things that no longer give you purpose – and accept new beginnings and learn to take risks.

But do not settle when you know that you are destined for more. Be the person who understands every inconsistency in life and who tries to make sense of their uncertainties, even if they cannot accept them. Be the person who is willing to take chances, on people, places and ideas, on adventures and new opportunities and relationships. Be the person who does not give up too easily, and when they do it is because they are open to the possibility of something different and new. Be the person who chooses to make a change. Be the person who appreciates the losses and the gains and every big and little hurdle that they must cross, because they understand that these highs and lows are what make life and living a worthwhile experience. Be the person who accepts growth, and who knows that sometimes life must descend into darkness before it can rise into the light again.

Be the person who accepts adventures and experiences, no matter how uncomfortable or foreign they may initially seem. Be the person who finds peace in their own company, the person who can sit with themselves for hours and not feel afraid of their own thoughts, of their own emotions or ideas. Be the person who chooses love, happiness and forgiveness. Be the person who chooses to be soft in the face of hatred, negativity and pain.

If they loved your soul, they would not have *left
it in pieces.*

At First Sight

I am fed up of hearing that love happens straight away – at first sight. That is just attraction. And if that turns into something more later then that potentially can be love, but not the feeling you had the moment that you saw them. Do not rate the strength of your love based on feelings of jitteriness that you receive when you think about them. Rate it based on friendship, trust, companionship, understanding, and the extent to which they make you happy. And by happy I do not mean a state of mind at a time but a state of being, a state of living. Love is not something that makes you feel out of this world all the time. It makes you feel out of the world, yes, but it also grounds you. It also brings you closer to your imperfect self rather than keep you in a fictitious fairy-tale where everything is wonderful and perfect.

Love is beautiful, yes. Love is out of this world, yes. But love is also consistent and long-lasting. And that is not dependent on the number of butterflies that flutter in your stomach but the overall value that it adds to your life. It is real only when it is durable, not when it is a momentary feeling of ecstasy.

All the Wrong Places

You must stop searching for happiness in all the wrong places. You must stop looking inside shallow souls with empty hearts, in hope that you will find love for yourself in there. You must stop searching for your reflection in eyes that can never see how much you shine, in eyes that will never understand the reason why you bloom. You cannot keep looking for potential in others, because you need to see them for who they truly are. And I know that you find hope in them, despite the anxiety, the discomfort and the sadness that they cause you to feel. I know that you want to see the good in them, but this is wrong. Others do not have the same heart as you, and that is the truth. And you can try and try but you will never be able to change someone or mold them to their potential or fix them.

You must stop searching for happiness in those who do not know how to truly keep you happy. You must stop building homes in the hearts of those whose doors will never open for you. If they wanted to treat you right, they would. If they wanted to keep you in their life, they would. If they wanted to seat you beside them rather than let you walk away, they would grip you tightly by the hand, believe me – they would. It is as simple as that. You cannot make someone care about you and you cannot make them stay.

Because believe me, if they wanted to stay – they would.

You Will Get There

Believe me, you will get there. One day, you will wake up on a lazy Sunday morning with the love of your life fast asleep by your side, and you will prop up on your elbows and drop a soft kiss on their forehead before sliding out of bed to greet the day. At that point, everything will fall into place. You will not worry about racing through life, instead you will take it steadily – you will let the sun be kind to your skin, just as your lover is to your heart. And you will smile, wholeheartedly, unabashedly, the kind of smile that spreads from cheek to cheek and does not leave as the day pushes forward. You will laugh and dance and feel giddy with joy, but you will not view life as the warmest journey. You will accept that life is not easy, and that love is the toughest commitment you could make, but you will appreciate the hard corners and rawness that your experiences will bring you.

You will know that even on days when darkness presses down on your back and your heart thumps with sorrow – love, a positive sense of self-worth, family and friendship; they can all save you. One day, you will wrap your arms around the love of your life and drop a kiss on their shoulder, not for saving you, not for holding your hand to steady you, not for being the air that you breathe in, but for standing beside you while you continue to do all those things for yourself, every single day.

Look at you – hurting, breaking and grieving *over and over again,* but still living, still healing and still growing through it *over and over again.*

Dear Heart (Part 2)

Dear heart, things are not as easy as I thought they would be. Life is often blotchy with light and dark and sometimes the darkness is more, and the light a lot less. This healing journey is not as easy as I assumed and, more often than not, my heart is carried by new hands into the unseen, into the unknown. By hands that do not know how to be gentle with my feelings, my thoughts and my wounds, hands that do not know anything other than how to love roughly, or barely, or not at all. It is difficult, dear heart. It is difficult being soft in a world that pushes you to the brink of hardness, in a world that does not appreciate the tenderness of people who just want to love and be loved in return.

So, I want you to take things slowly. I want you to be vigilant, and I do not want you to trust people with ease once more. It is going to be an uncomfortable journey to be on, dear heart. One that is filled with several challenges where you must choose yourself over them, where you must put yourself first, where you must prioritize your self-worth, because I know you do not feel things in that way. I know that you hurt for others more than you hurt for yourself. I know that you put a lot more care into giving others what they deserve without worrying whether they will treat you right. But I want you to start putting yourself first. I want you to let reason take the rein of my actions sometimes without worrying too much about whether I will lose the one thing that makes me, me – which is you.

And if you cannot, if you find yourself struggling with rationality taking control, if you think it is too tough for me to think from my mind rather than follow you, then just do me this one favor. Dear heart, I want you to stop feeling things for a while.

Listen To Your Gut

Sometimes your gut tells you things that your heart refuses to hear. Your gut churns your insides with an anxious feeling that you cannot push away, no matter how hard you try and all I ask of you is to hear what it has to say. I know you want to believe that despite the odds, the red signals, the hurt, the pain and the constant confusion – they could be the one. But you need to listen to that soft but stern voice at the back of your head that tells you to recognize reality. You need to stop looking for potential in people, and you need to stop gazing at them through a rose-tinted lens that paints them as perfect and see them as they truly are instead.

Observe the way that they treat you, focus on how they make you feel, acknowledge how much effort they put into making sure you are safe and okay in their presence and take your time, because you must. And if they hurt you or say things that cause a bell to ring at the back of your head, telling you that something is wrong – hear it out. Our gut is often right in all cases where our heart is wrong, and we need to rely on it if we are to protect ourselves from temporary people and hurtful situations. Love and feelings are beautiful when you initially fall into them, but red signals are a real thing. So, focus on them and pay attention to everything that feels wrong even when everything is right. Believe me, if you listen your gut – it will protect your heart in ways you never imagined.

Learn to let go of the ones that never loved you *to make room* for those who will.

It is Not Love

It is not love if it causes you to question your self-worth, if it lowers your dignity or if it makes you feel like you are not worth loving. It is not love if you cry yourself to sleep each night, if it causes you to feel insecure, and if it makes you sad rather than happy. It is not love if it has given you more sorrow and grief than love is supposed to, if all it ever does is throb painfully in your chest, and if it makes you wish that things were different.

It is not love if it wraps itself around your ankles like chains and you cannot walk forward with it, and if it does not hold your hand but grips your wrist instead. It is not love if it feels heavy in your heart, if it makes you feel like a stranger in your own body and if it does not let you think about the future, because all you can think about is the past. It is not love if every dream you had about love does not come true, and if it feels more like a nightmare that you cannot seem to get through.

And it is never love if it makes you feel like you made a mistake by getting into it, if it makes you feel like you were wrong – just because you fell in love.

Irreplaceable

We all have at least one person in our lives who is completely irreplaceable. You cannot find someone like them anywhere. There is something about them, but you cannot place your finger on what it is. Perhaps it is their aura, or spirit, or their heart. Whatever it is, you know in the deepest depths of your soul that you can search every single corner of the earth and still not find another 'them'. And if they left, you know that you would lose a gem. But we should not let this thought, or the actuality of it, bring us down or break us. Their presence or absence in your life as this incredible person who cannot be replaced should not be a misfortune on your part, but a success on theirs. A person like this should be celebrated, regardless of whether they are still present in your life. A person like this, no matter where they go, will shine light upon the lives of all those around them.

I know that losing someone irreplaceable feels like a tragic loss but having the good fortune of experiencing such a magnificent person in your life – even if it was for a short while – is something you should be grateful for. Trust me, there is no harm in admitting to yourself that some people cannot be replaced, but you should do it with a smile. So, the next time you are asked if there is, or was, someone irreplaceable in your life – say it with the kind of grin that makes your face glow. For, you should be proud to have met a person during your finite existence who reached this pedestal, one that can never be matched.

Walk Away

Sometimes you are not confused about the other person – you are scared. You are scared that even if you let your walls down, they might not. You are scared that maybe you will let them in, maybe you will show them your fears, your insecurities, your blemishes, your hopes and dreams, your weakness and your darkness – but they will not do the same. Or perhaps they will not like what they see. Perhaps they will look at you, after you have removed every layer of yourself, and they will no longer see the beautiful person whom they thought you were. You are scared that you will let them in and, just when you begin to trust them, they will break your trust and hurt your soul. You are scared that you might begin to love someone again, you might begin to let your heart feel things that it has not felt for so long – but they will not appreciate it, they will not value your softness or your emotions, and they might just let you go.

Sometimes you are not confused about whether they are the one – you are scared that what if they are, what if they are everything that you have been searching for, but they do not feel the same way about you. You are scared that you will jump off your lifeboat into the uncertainty of love – and they will break your heart and walk away.

All you need to do is take a step forward, all you
need to do is embrace life. Just like you always
have *every time someone walked away.*

The Previous Year

The previous year was bitter-sweet, and I learned more than I could imagine. Each cold morning faded into a delicate summer's day and I made friends, the kind who taught me about life and happiness and healing. I visited new places, watching the sun set behind torn buildings in one city and rise by the ocean in another. I watched time pass in small cafés tucked away into the pleats of busy streets with a book, coffee and myself for company. I tasted salty water and felt the sand find a home beneath my toes as I walked into self-discovery. I danced on the streets with my loved ones and shared stories as night turned into day. I walked on foreign land and uncovered foreign parts of myself, in hope to become more at one. I found love in new ways – in the form of friendship and family, in the form of a person who felt like sunlight on the darkest days of the year. I read books that taught me about self-love, I watched movies that took me into new worlds, I listened to music that soothed the ache inside my chest.

I shed parts of myself and gained new parts; parts that were wiser, kinder, fiercer, bolder, and parts that roared in new ways. I found happiness in my own arms and in the arms of people who settled inside my soul. I discovered friendship. The kind that leaves you smiling at the memory of easy experiences and endless laughter for years to come. I also lost friendship, the kind of loss that leaves you feeling hollow, as though you have lost a huge part of yourself. I spent days out on adventures with people who left a huge smile on my face, and I made countless memories that will hold me through all the tough times that are yet to come in my life. But I also cried and cried until my heart could not take it anymore. I remembered lost love and dipped into old sorrow, and I also found new love. I discovered myself and other people and I realized what I needed from life. I healed and moved and walked forward, but I also stopped and stumbled and fell. I received more love from people who kept me going, and the arms of delicate souls continued to lift me up.

The previous year was bitter-sweet, where I loved and gained more than I could imagine, but I also learned, lost and forgave.

Same Person

I know that you have been made to feel like you are not enough time and time again. You have been shown by more actions and less words that somehow your feelings were not valid, that somehow you felt too much, but still you were never enough, that somehow you loved too much, but still you were never enough. I know it hurts to think that the people you cared about the most never truly realized your depths. They could not understand what made you so special, they could not appreciate your beauty. And the worst thing is, when they did realize – it was too late. Your heart no longer wanted them, and your smile no longer depended on their existence.

I guess that is the harsh truth of life. Sometimes people finally appreciate you and realize what they lost – but only when it is too late. And no matter how hard you try to start off from where you left, and no matter how badly you want to take them back with open arms – your heart no longer loves them. And no matter how much you want to keep the past close to you, sometimes people come back and there is no space left in your life for them. Sometimes people come back, and you cannot love them in the same way again. Sometimes people come back, and you wish they hadn't because now you do not know where to place them in your life. And sometimes, the only way to understand it all is to think that even though they came back to you – you were no longer the same person they had left to begin with.

According to Plan

You must accept that life will not always go according to plan, but that does not mean that what is happening is not supposed to happen. What I am trying to say is this – life is completely unexpected in the most wonderful way and that is because whatever is meant to happen will happen, and sometimes that is not what you want, but that is the beauty of it. You can will certain things into action, but the remaining will always be governed by the laws of nature acting in a way that promotes your wellbeing. At the time you experience things, you may not appreciate what is going on because you might feel that the gods above or the natural laws are against you, but really, over time you will realize that everything that takes place slowly fuels your growth.

What is meant to be will be, and this is something we need to understand. We need to accept that sometimes our wishes will not be granted but that is because something better is envisioned for us, and we need to accept that our plan may not always work because there is a plan much bigger than us that incorporates us all. And we need to accept the most important thing – that what does not break us only makes us stronger, and that is what the lesson should be. We must find strength within our scars and we must search for light in the dark and if we cannot find it – we must become the light. And we must keep going, we must keep going.

It is not loving that you should be afraid of – it is
giving your love to the wrong person.
That is what the lesson should be, and that is all that
you should be taking from heartbreak.

Let Them Go

No one has the right to make you feel as though you are not enough. As though you are too fat or too skinny, or too tall or too short, or perhaps you are not as good looking as those they compare you to. No one has the right to make you feel like you fall short of just what they are searching for, like somehow you do not have the qualities that they want, or the personality that they appreciate. You are complete in yourself. You are worthy of love, kindness and companionship. And if someone does not feel that way about you, if they look at you and do not welcome the truth that your imperfections make you just as beautiful as your positive traits do, if they think that they can do better than you, if they cannot absorb your magnificence – then you must hold the door for them, head held high, shoulders wide, without an ounce of sadness on your face as they leave.

You are not here to please other people or to live up to their standards of beauty and perfection. You are not here to frame yourself in another's image of who is worth loving. You are here for you. If you feel beautiful, no one else has the right to tell you otherwise. If you know that you are more than enough, no one else has the right to make you feel differently. And if they do, if they try to change you or reduce your self-worth, if they want to adapt you so that you can fit into their concept of 'beauty' or their idea of 'perfection' – then you must hug yourself as tightly as you can, because that is when you know that it is time to let them go.

Learn to Hold On

Love is hard, but life even more so. This unsteady line of growth that weathers your soft parts as time passes, that hardens your edges and pushes you to the rawness of strength. You tackle each day with fists bunched up at your sides and a wary expression on your face for what the day will hold. And sometimes you pass through it, sometimes the sun forms a soft aura around you and people are kind to your heart and your bones are not tired as the day pushes forward. Sometimes there are ears that listen to your thoughts, there are hands that comfort your back and your mind does not thump hard with memories of a past long gone. But sometimes, you must gather the courage to face the darkness alone.

On those days, the only thing that will listen to your worries is your own soul, the only hand you will be able to hold will be the one that has always wiped away your tears, the one that comforts you when the arms of others are no longer there. On those days, life falls heavy on you, with its rigid lessons and harsh reality. On those days, you must learn to find beauty in the rawness of pain. Sometimes life breezes past gently, and sometimes, you cannot spend another moment alone. It is on those days that you must learn to be strong, it is on those days that you must learn to hold on.

Feeling Things this Deeply

It is exhausting having the kind of heart that melts for those who show it the tiniest amount of love. It is exhausting trying to break down stone walls that belong to others when your own soul craves to be held. It is exhausting constantly justifying other people's ill-treatment of you, just because you are a good person, just because you think that you understand why they are acting in this way, just because you think that you can change them with your love. It is exhausting carrying your heart on your sleeve, as though it is not your most prized possession, as though it is not the most beautiful jewel that others need to earn before they can touch it, as though your heart is not already fragmented and torn by those who came and left before.

It is exhausting being affected by people more than needed, and for breaking, for hurting, for shattering time and time again – just because you wanted to help, just because you thought they had some hope left within them, just because they said things that insinuated that they needed you, that they wanted you. It is exhausting trying to heal others when you are the one who needs to lean on the wall of strength to journey torwards the light, when you are the one who has been hurt more than words can fathom, when you are the one that needs to keep going, to keep learning, and to keep healing.

And it is exhausting, believe me, it is so exhausting feeling things this deeply all the time when all you wish for is to shut off for a little while. When all you pray for is a little bit of solace from the pain. Because it is exhausting, believe me, it is so exhausting.

You must stop counting the reasons why other people should be loved and start appreciating the many reasons *why you are the one* who is worth loving.

Meant to Be

We tend to find a cause or a reason for everything that we experience, whether good or bad. This is especially the case when it comes to experiences that hurt us, or things that do not work out the way we wanted them to – like broken relationships. Often, we blame ourselves or the person whom we were with as being the cause for our failed relationship. *'She did not understand me', or 'He did not love me as much as I did'*. These explanations are fine to use, and they are understandable because perhaps that is what happened.

But perhaps things did not work out because they were not meant to be. It is simple, but most of us find it so difficult to understand. Sometimes it is not you or them who is at fault. Sometimes no one is at fault. The suffering that you both endured was not a result of your inconsistencies or their flaws, but circumstances. No one was to blame other than the situation that you both found yourself in, other than the experiences that you both had that resulted in your fallen relationship. And that is all. You do not need to find a reason or a cause for why it did not work out, although being human and tending to find reasons for your suffering to give it meaning forces you to. But your explanation will not change the truth – that the laws of nature interplayed in such a way that you both were not meant to be.

'Meant to be' – it is easy to understand this phrase when relationships work out, but we find it hard to accept it in cases when things do not work out. Instead, we resort to blaming each other, we find reasons that probably did not exist to begin with because the pain makes sense then.

Our experiences, both good and bad, do not always need to fit in with our worldview, we do not need to make sense of our pain or suffering in a rational manner every time and, sometimes, there is no reason other than the fact that it was not meant to be. And the sooner we accept that this is why things went wrong, the better it is for us because otherwise we would spend our whole lives trying and failing to understand what truly happened. It was not meant to be – it is as simple and as clear as could be.

You Are Beautiful

I think that you are beautiful. I think that you are beautiful in the way you hold yourself against all odds. Your eyes gleam with self-love and affirmation, despite the questioning glares of others, despite the negativity that some experiences bring, despite the hurdles, both high and low, despite the mental and emotional turmoil you often find yourself in, and the disordered nature of life in all its shades. I think that you are beautiful when you do not feel beautiful. When you look at yourself in the mirror and notice the tiny imperfections that adorn you like jewels, the blemishes and the scars and all your tender curves and hard edges, and your lips arch up into a thin smile that does not reach your eyes – you do not feel beautiful or perfect or enough, but for me, that is when beauty engulfs you the most.

I think that you are beautiful because of your mind. The clutter of your thoughts challenge me and push boundaries that I never knew existed. Your mind enthralls and intrigues me and graces you with an intellectual maturity that I did not know existed. I think that you are beautiful because of your heart, it gently flows with kindness and love, and it gives and gives until there is nothing left for itself. But your heart does not harden because of this, it has unbounded space for others and chooses to keep only a little bit for itself.

The most beautiful thing about you are your eyes – they shine with both strength and fragility, and even though they shed more tears of sadness than they do of happiness, they never fall short of sprinkling affection everywhere that you go. I think that you are beautiful when you are trying not to be. Because that is when your beauty is effortless, that is when I can see it the most. When you try not to be anything other than yourself; untamed, soft and gentle, and flawed but in a magical way – that is when you appear the most beautiful to me.

Choose Your Heart

Practicing self-love is hard. Heck, it is one of the hardest things that I have learned to do. Waking up each morning as the sun splinters through the comfort of your blinds, shaking you to the reality that even though you do not want to get up, the day has begun without you. Wrapping yourself tightly with strength and dignity, just so you can walk through paths stuffed with lessons as each day unfolds. Lessons in the form of all kinds of people – those who can never learn to appreciate you, those who love you toxically, those who care about you but for them you will never be perfect, those who cannot appreciate your journey or your purpose, those who only know how to give love to you but whom you can never give anything to in return, and those who are there for you throughout it all and will never leave your side, even if you leave them.

Loving yourself is difficult. Especially when you have been taught your whole life that perhaps you are not enough, that perhaps you need to work harder on the way you look or the emotions you feel. But that is the beauty of the journey. If we had known everything about self-love since we were young, then we would not have to learn about it – and the learning is what allows us to grow. Yes, I wish we could all appreciate ourselves and love our imperfections as much as our perfections from the onset, but life is not perfect and most of us have been taught to tug at our blemishes and flaws rather than welcome them and the stories they tell.

So, we must learn to love ourselves if we are to survive in a world that tells us otherwise. We must clench our fists with our vulnerabilities enclosed tightly in our palms. We must stride forward with the string of self-love twirled around our tired hearts and we must accept the aching, the experiences and the journey. And we must remember that it is okay to be imperfect in a blemished world. We can still love ourselves, we can still be happy, we can still heal, smile and soar through life, and we can continue to choose our hearts over and over again.

We must *find strength within our scars*
and search for light in the dark and if we cannot find
it – we must become the light and *we must keep
going,* we must keep going.

Let This Be the Year

Let this be the year that you welcome your growth and you become unafraid of making mistakes. Let this be the year that you find strength within your wounds, worn out by experiences that taught you countless things about life, and that you trace every imperfection of yours as a reason to feel beautiful. Let this be the year that you recognize your pain and embrace it as a part of you, that you stop reprimanding yourself every time you get hurt thinking about the past, because it makes you feel like you have not moved on. Let this be the year that you finally accept that to be vulnerable is to be brave, to be broken is to love honestly and to be scared is to be human.

Let this be the year that you learn to live with your grief by your side and you do not rush your healing journey, and you give yourself as many chances, if not more, than you give others. Let this be the year that you stop saying 'yes' to everyone and start saying 'no' for yourself, to save yourself, to prevent from losing parts of your heart that you will never get back. Let this be the year that you realize how wrong it is to neglect yourself because others made you feel unworthy. Let this be the year that you hug your broken pieces and spill love into all the cracks that people left inside you, and you begin to hold yourself together, no matter who wants to pull you apart.

Let this be the year that you fall crazy in love with a wonderful human being. Let this be the year that you open your arms, your heart and your soul wide to let love in with all its intensity. Let this be the year that you put your happiness first and you experience, appreciate and breathe in life in all its different shades. Let this be the year that you stop thinking that you are not good enough and start counting the ways in which you are beautiful and magnificent, the year you accept that you are a miracle. Let this be the year that you grasp that not just getting hurt but also hurting other people is a part of being human and you stop being so hard on yourself because of it.

Let this be the year that you start making a change to better your life, and you discover your journey and the many lessons you have learned. Let this be the year that everything makes sense, the year that all the pieces finally come together.

Let this be your year, just yours.

Thank you for reading pieces of my soul, I hope they comforted the ache in yours.

About the Author

Ruby Dhal is a British South-Asian writer and author of three books of poetry and prose. After experiencing her mother's death at the tender age of 4, Ruby battled with various negative emotions. Growing up, she turned to books as a form of escapism from painful experiences of the real world. Ruby's love for reading and writing grew over the years, allowing her to understand the healing power of books. She realized that books brought readers closer to the real world instead of pushing them away, and that is how she came to understand and accept her true self. Ruby's only dream is to become an established novelist one day.

In January 2016, Ruby created a poetry page on Instagram to heal from a few hurtful experiences she underwent, and within a few months, Ruby's page gained incredible momentum. 3 years later, Ruby has a generous readership of over 260,000 people on Instagram, Twitter and Facebook. Ruby's social media following is swiftly increasing and her passion for writing to heal and allow her readers to acknowledge, accept and come to terms with their emotions on their healing journey has allowed Ruby to receive an endless amount of love and support from her readers.

Ruby also writes for We Are the Tempest and the Thought Catalog on the same themes that she shares on her social media pages – love, heartbreak, mental health, healing, relationships, self-discovery and self-worth. Presently, Ruby is working on her debut novel which is a contemporary thriller romance and endeavors to find a home for it in the Fall of 2020.

You can find Ruby on Instagram (@r.dhalwriter), Facebook (@r.dhalwriter) and Twitter (@rdhalwriter).